LIVING FAITHFULLY IN A FRAGMENTED WORLD

NML NEW MONASTIC LIBRARY
Resources for Radical Discipleship

For over a millennium, if Christians wanted to read theology, practice Christian spirituality, or study the Bible, they went to the monastery to do so. There, people who inhabited the tradition and prayed the prayers of the church also copied manuscripts and offered fresh reflections about living the gospel in a new era. Two thousand years after the birth of the church, a new monastic movement is stirring in North America. In keeping with ancient tradition, new monastics study the classics of Christian reflection and are beginning to offer some reflections for a new era. The New Monastic Library includes reflections from new monastics as well as classic monastic resources unavailable elsewhere.

Series Editor: Jonathan Wilson-Hartgrove

Living Faithfully in a
FRAGMENTED WORLD

From
After Virtue
to a
New
Monasticism

SECOND EDITION

JONATHAN R. WILSON

CASCADE *Books* · Eugene, Oregon

LIVING FAITHFULLY IN A FRAGMENTED WORLD
From *After Virtue* to a New Monasticism
Second Edition

New Monastic Library: Resources for Radical Discipleship (NML) 6

Cascade Books
An Imprint of Wipf and Stock Publishers
199 W. 8th Ave., Suite 3
Eugene, OR 97401

www.wipfandstock.com

ISBN 13: 978-1-55635-898-2

Cataloging-in-Publication data:

Wilson, Jonathan R.

Living faithfully in a fragmented world : from After Virtue to a new monasticism / Jonathan R. Wilson.

xx + 82 p. ; 23 cm. —Includes bibliographical references.

New Monastic Library: Resources for Radical Discipleship (NML) 6

ISBN 13: 978-1-55635-898-2

1. Mission of the church. 2. Church and the world. 3. Christian ethics. 4. Culture conflict—Moral and ethical aspects. 5. Culture conflict—United States—History—20th century. 6. United States—Moral conditions. I. Title. II. Series.

BV601.8 .W49 2010

CONTENTS

ACKNOWLEDGMENTS

Many friends have contributed to this work. I first learned to read MacIntyre from Stanley Hauerwas and Thomas Spragens Jr. at Duke University. There also, a wonderful group of graduate students contributed to my thinking. Klaus Bockmuehl, now with the Lord, helped me crystallize what I wanted to say about MacIntyre for an essay in *CRUX*, of which he was then the editor. Don Lewis, who succeeded Klaus as editor of *CRUX*, then published the essay (Wilson, 1990). That essay prompted Wilbert Shenk to invite me to expand the argument of the essay for Trinity Press International's Christian Mission and Modern Culture series. I am grateful to him for the invitation. I am also indebted to the many questions raised in response to that essay by Philip Rolnick and Thomas Langford that forced me to think further about these issues. Professor MacIntyre kindly read that early essay and corrected some errors and misrepresentations that it contained.

I am indebted to Dean George V. Blankenbaker and the Professional Development Committee of Westmont College for granting me a semester's sabbatical during which I completed the first edition.

My wife, Marti Crosby, and our daughter, Leah, have been a constant source of encouragement for my writing, but, more importantly, for living faithfully. I owe much to their loving discipline. Since I wrote the first edition of this book, Leah has married Jonathan Wilson-Hartgrove. Their vision and calling and living has given embodiment to the words of this text and shown me and many others what the Spirit is doing among us. It is a joy to see faith in Christ live from one generation to the next as I dedicate this book to my father, J. Reford Wilson (1924–95) and my mother, M. Gene Wilson, who have faithfully given their lives in witness to the Gospel.

When I wrote the first edition of *Living Faithfully in a Fragmented World*, I did not know that it was about a new monastic movement. I did not even mention new monasticism or MacIntyre's anticipation of "another—doubtless very different—St. Benedict" in the *CRUX* article that generated the invitation to write the book. But as I wrote the first edition of this book and came to the end of *After Virtue*, I realized that MacIntyre's cryptic remark in the closing sentence of his book provided a fifth lesson for the church. My last chapter on "New Monasticism," then, became something of an appendix to the earlier, more developed exposition of MacIntyre's contribution to the church's living faithfully in a fragmented world.

Until 2003. That year my son-in-law, Jonathan Wilson-Hartgrove, browsed through *Living Faithfully* as he thought about his final project for a course in Christian Hospitality taught by Margaret Kim Peterson. He connected the chapter on new monasticism and the practice of Christian hospitality with the vision and calling that had been guiding my daughter for five years. All of that came together under the guidance of the Holy Spirit as Leah and Jonathan committed themselves to establishing a new monastic community of hospitality in Durham, North Carolina, where Jonathan would be attending Duke Divinity School. It was then that Leah and Jonathan moved to the Walltown Neighborhood of Durham and helped establish the Rutba House.

In 2004, Jonathan used a grant from the Fund for Theological Education to gather people together to consider the call to a new monasticism. After that gathering, a lively network of new monastic communities developed through connections to long-established communities (including the Benedictines) and through the establishment of new communities.

The vision and energy of these communities and their embrace of the vision for a new monasticism calls for continuing discernment of God's guidance for new monastic communities, threats and pitfalls that we face, and those things necessary for sustaining faithfulness in our life together and before the watching world.

This new edition of *Living Faithfully* seeks to provide those resources for new monastic communities. Now that I know that the book is about new monasticism from beginning to end, it seemed good to rewrite it extensively in order to direct the exposition and argument of every chapter toward the call for a new monasticism.

This new edition is also an opportunity to develop the vision for a new monasticism, respond to criticisms, and correct misunderstandings. Since the publication of *Living Faithfully* and the increasing visibility of new monastics, the media have given some attention to the movement—newspapers, radio programs, television, and magazines have been intrigued. This coverage presents a problem of discernment for new monastics.

Since new monasticism is rooted in a stringent critique of modernity and postmodernity, it must be very wary of its relationship to institutions that are so deeply shaped by those cultures. In addition, since new monasticism is committed in its essence to building local community and serving locally, it has to resist becoming dissipated by wider exposure. Its ministry and witness are local.

At the same time, part of the argument of this book is that the church needs the life and witness of new monastic communities to learn to live with its history, expose the failure of the Enlightenment project, explain the contingency of its collapse into postmodernity so that postmodernity loses its veneer of inevitability and inescapability, recover a more coherent life of discipleship, and learn the gospel more fully. So doesn't all of that call for a larger witness than the local? Isn't access to the media part of fulfilling the mission of the new monastics?

The way through this tension is a process of discernment—of practical moral reasoning engaged in by communities that are seeking to be well formed. In the early years of community formation, most energy should be directed locally. Communities will take some time to mature and to live into their rule and their life together. The practices of discernment need to be developed in relation to local relationships and tasks—local meaning not only the new monastic community but also its neighbors, friends, and church. So part of the discernment process in relation to media interest will be to discern whether a new monastic community is mature enough to even consider a media inquiry. Here the network of new monastic communities should be a resource as a new monastic community consults with another community to discern its calling in a particular instance.

In addition to the tension that exists between the mission of new monastics and the interests of the media, the actual content of media coverage presents a challenge for new monastics. One of the biggest challenges, especially within the evangelical community, is to differentiate the new monastics from the Christian communes of the 1960s and 1970s. Most of those communities were short-lived. Many may suspect that new monastic communities will be short-lived too. That is certainly possible, and even if it is the case this movement may still be of God and may have a long-lasting impact should the new monastic communities disappear.

But there are some important differences between those Christian communes and the new monastics. First, most of the communes of the 60s and 70s retreated from the culture into geographically isolated, inward-turning life. It is instructive that two of those early communities that have thrived—Jesus People USA (J-PUSA) and Reba Place Fellowship—thrust themselves into the midst of the culture and engaged in holistic mission. These are both marks of new monasticism. So it is a profound misunderstanding of the new monastics to identify them with the separatist mentality of communes of the 60s and 70s. New monastics are living intentional, disciplined lives in response to a critique of the culture, but the nature of that critique, and more importantly their understanding of the gospel, lead them more deeply into the culture and into mission in the midst of the world, not into a geographical isolation and purist withdrawal from the world.

A second difference between the communes and the new monastics is their relation to the church. For the communes, their way of life was rooted in a rejection of "the establishment," including the church. For the new monastics, their movement is marked by "humble submission to Christ's body, the church." This submission may take many different forms and because of the looseness of the movement may not consistently be practiced everywhere and always. But the commitment is there and the various communities do seek to hold one another accountable to this commitment.

A third difference between these two movements is their motivation. This is admittedly difficult to discern with certainty. However, it seems relatively clear to me that the communes were often rooted in an idealistic, thinly Christianized Age-of-Aquarius mentality. By contrast, the new monastics are grounded in a realism about their own sinfulness that comes from the ancient practices of the church.[1] They are also schooled by John Perkins and others in realism about the kind of life and the time that are required to be faithful to God's calling to a particular place. This schooling connects directly with a new monastic vow of stability.

In addition to differentiating the new monastics from Christian communes of the 60s and 70s, it is also important to continually address the accusation that the call to new monastic communities is a withdrawal from the church's call to mission in the world. I anticipated this accusation in the first edition of *Living Faithfully* when I wrote, "this call to a new monasticism may sound irresponsible. Some will label such a vision 'sectarian.'"[2] I then sought to disarm this accusation—or at least provide a context for a good argument about the allegation of irresponsible withdrawal. Nevertheless, the accusation is made—and made without due attention to my argument.

In a long footnote, D. A. Carson makes the following claim:

> Even though Wilson revises MacIntyre's appeal to a "new monasticism," the resulting picture is of a separatist community, a sort of updated Anabaptist community. Speaking of tradition, that is one of only several possible models that appeal to Scripture to justify a set of relations between church and the broader culture. Doubtless the best-known typology is the five-fold scheme of H. Richard Niebuhr, *Christ and Culture* (New York: Harper & Row, 1956). Wilson's adoption of one of those patterns without wrestling with whether or not any of the other four might have equal or better claim to biblical warrant is doubtless prompted by the fact that, as he himself attests, he first learned to read MacIntyre under the tutelage of Stanley Hauerwas. For myself, I am inclined to think that all five patterns are found in Scripture but that each is tied to peculiar historical circumstances. I defend this view in a forthcoming publication.[3]

1. Several of the new monastics learned this discipline from Chris Hall, professor of Theology at Eastern University.

2. Wilson, *Living Faithfully* (1997), 71.

3. Carson, *Becoming Conversant*, 146.

Before addressing the specific critique of new monasticism in this quote, two preliminary concerns must be cleared away. First, the appeal to Niebuhr is problematic in light of the criticisms that have been rightly directed toward his work. The helpfulness of Niebuhr's typology and of his descriptions of the types is highly contested today.[4] For Carson to simply assign "new monasticism" to Niebuhr's "Christ against culture" type neglects the nuance I offer in my exposition. Secondly, it is wrong for Carson to be "doubtless" about why I do not consider the other four options that Niebuhr offers. Indeed, at one level it is offensive to suggest that I come to the conclusions that I do because I am "under the tutelage of Stanley Hauerwas." I am honored to be associated with Hauerwas and join with him in our concern for the church's life and witness to the gospel, but for Carson to suggest that I have not thought about these matters or to hint that I have no reasons for my argument or position other than Stanley Hauerwas's influence is a clever and vicious put-down that is unworthy of a trained exegete who should know "the personalist heresy" and recognize it in his own writing.

Now to the matter that is most directly relevant to "new monasticism" —the observation that it leads to "a separatist community." Although I made a number of comments about the strategic, tactical, and contingent elements of the need for a new monasticism in *Living Faithfully* (70–72), I think I think I left open—slightly—the possibility that new monastic communities could develop into isolated, quietistic communities that seek to establish and maintain their purity, to maintain some sort of barrier between themselves and the wider culture in a quest to establish and maintain their purity. But such a quest is unfaithful to the vision that the entire book lays out. It is for the sake of the mission of the church, and thus for the sake of the world, that God is calling new monastic communities into being. So if their life is not completed in mission, then they are not faithful to God's. It is also the case that only a very narrow and tendentious understanding of "Anabaptist community" could be useful to Carson in this context.

In Carson's footnote he wonders why I do not consider the alternatives in Niebuhr's typology. I do not directly consider those other types partly because I think that Niebuhr's entire project is misleading; to take

---

4. Stassen et al., *Authentic Transformation*; Gustafson, "Preface"; Carter, *Rethinking*; Stackhouse, *Making*. D. A. Carson himself provides a more nuanced account of these matters in his later work (2008).

it as a point of departure misdirects the discussion from the beginning. In my text, I argue quite clearly that the call for a new monasticism is directly related to the entire forgoing analysis of our culture and my theological reframing of MacIntyre's argument. (I was thinking of 2 Cor 10: 1–6 while writing the book. My intent was to emulate Paul.) I do think that we may discern God working in many different ways in the world, but I also believe that given the argument of *After Virtue* and the lessons of *Living Faithfully*, we need new monastic communities to discern those ways because so much of the church's life is compromised and co-opted by a culture that is anti-Christ.[5]

This book is written under the conviction that the church in Western culture is in grave danger of compromising its faithfulness to the gospel. Of course, such conviction is almost always present somewhere in the church. Nevertheless, because of the enormous changes that are taking place in our culture, such conviction takes on greater significance. This book is also written under the conviction that the changes taking place in Western culture present a wonderful opportunity for faithful witness to the gospel, as the church in the West reexamines its own life and witness and discovers once again the power of the gospel of Jesus Christ to redeem humanity.

Guided by these twin convictions, I describe in this book several aspects of contemporary culture that create both opportunities for, and threats to, Christian mission. On the basis of this description, I suggest some understandings and practices that the church must adopt today in order to live faithfully and witness effectively to the gospel of Jesus Christ.

I have also had some opportunities to present this material to people who are engaged in ministry outside the domination of Western culture and have heard from them the relevance of these lessons even for their mission. In June 2006, I taught a cohort of DMin students— North American and South American—who are engaged in ministry in Bolivia. As something of a test case, I presented this material to them in a lecture. They found the material highly illuminating for their context. They especially saw the call to new monastic communities as one that fit

---

5. One of the oddest accusations directed toward *Living Faithfully* is Carson's conclusion that "In the hands of Wilson and McLaren . . . MacIntyre becomes a voice in defense of a post-modern agenda." Since this accusation is at most tangentially related to new monasticism, I have addressed it in an Appendix to this book.

their cultural context and the need of the church for more disciplined living. In several courses I have taught students whose ministries are primarily contextualized by immigrants from mainland China or who work primarily in mainland China. They too find the lessons here illuminating and fitting for their context. Such is the power of MacIntyre's analysis.[6]

Beyond the power of MacIntyre's analysis is the power of Jesus Christ. His call to faithful living and witness is given to the church in the "Great Commission":

> And Jesus came and said to them, "All authority in heaven and on earth has been given to me. Go therefore and make disciples of all nations, baptizing them in the name of the Father and of the Son and of the Holy Spirit, and teaching them to obey everything that I have commanded you. And remember, I am with you always, to the end of the age." (Matt 28:18–20)

In this passage, Jesus Christ calls the church to particular practices: making disciples, baptizing and teaching them. In the midst of much discussion about the relationship between these various practices, one thing is clear: their point of reference is the good news of Jesus Christ. This good news is an ever-present, unchanging reality: Jesus himself promises to be with us always. So the gospel which the church is commissioned to proclaim is not something we merely conjure up from the past or hope for in the future, though it certainly has a past and a future. Rather, the redemption of Jesus Christ is a present reality that he is actively accomplishing in our world today. Therefore, the church's responsibility is to participate in that redemption and witness to it. We are witnesses to Jesus Christ, ambassadors of God's reconciliation which is being accomplished through Christ. This responsibility extends to all peoples, to bring the gospel to them and educate them in the practices of the gospel—baptizing and teaching—so that they may participate in this redemption and become its witnesses.

This gospel and the mission of the church never change, but the circumstances in which we witness to and live out the gospel do change. With changing circumstances comes the need to rethink how the church lives faithfully and witnesses to the gospel. Changing circumstances bring new opportunities for witness, but they also bring new threats to the integrity

---

6. A Chinese translation of *Living Faithfully in a Fragmented World* was published in 2008. A Spanish translation of this book is planned.

of the church's witness. For example, Christians in some parts of Africa encounter the question of polygamy. Addressing this issue and shaping the life of the church to respond to this question provides an opportunity to live out the gospel in that situation, but it also threatens the possibility of unfaithfulness. We have recognized this same truth in situations closer to home. For example, how the church in the West handles the questions of divorce and remarriage is shaped by and shapes our understanding of the gospel. Sometimes the differences are more subtle, but still very significant: we know that a church in suburban Denver and one in downtown Denver face different challenges and look different. In other words, although the unchanging mission of the church is to witness to the good news of Jesus Christ, that witness must always discern the present reality of that redemption and shape the church's mission accordingly.

As I have noted above, the church faces many threats to its unfaithfulness. Words are important here: the *gospel* is never threatened by changing circumstances—God's purposes in Jesus Christ is being accomplished and nothing can hinder that. All authority has been given to Jesus Christ. However, what may be compromised is *the church's faithfulness to the gospel*. Even here, the church may be made a witness to Jesus Christ by God's judgment. That is, even an unfaithful church may be used to witness the gospel by God's judgment upon it. So what is at issue for us is not the gospel or our witness to the gospel, but the church's faithfulness to the commission given by Jesus Christ.

This understanding of the mission of the church must be disciplined by the gospel and firmly grounded in the conviction that "relevance" is an intrinsic characteristic of the gospel, not a demand of the culture. Otherwise, the quest for relevance becomes a quest for acceptance. As Julian Hartt reminds us, there is a great difference between the church asking the world, "Are you getting the message?" and asking the world, "Do you like the message?" or "Will you go on loving me even if you don't like my message?"[7]

Enormous changes are taking place in the culture within which we are called to witness. Although we have often been sensitive to changing circumstances due to changing places—from America to Africa, from suburban Denver to urban Denver—we have not always been aware of our own culture's historicity. Or, as I will later argue, when we have shown

---

7. Hartt, *Christian Critique*, 345.

some sensitivity to historical forces, we have often misread that history or indulged in a misplaced nostalgia. As a result of this neglect and misreading, the church is unprepared for the new challenges and opportunities that we face. We are in danger of failing to communicate the good news of Jesus Christ or of cloaking a nostalgia for the past in Christian language and mistaking its acceptance for acceptance of the gospel. The church is particularly vulnerable in times when a familiar and comfortable culture is changing. When a culture has been regnant for some time (even though there may be some minor changes along the way), it becomes familiar and the church develops strategies for faithful living and witness in that culture. But those established strategies may not be helpful in changing circumstances. Just as antibiotics aid the human body in resisting and conquering bacterial infections, but are ineffective against viral infections, so also strategies used by the church for living and witnessing faithfully in one culture may be ineffective in another culture.

At the present time, I believe that the church is in grave danger of compromising the gospel and the integrity of its witness by mistakenly relying on strategies that are not effective in our changing times. My concern is primarily with the church that is situated in Western culture—the culture of Europe and North America. As we move toward a global culture dominated by the technologies and economies of this culture, my concern becomes increasingly global. Nevertheless, as I will later argue, the church in "Western culture" faces particular challenges that arise from the history of its impact on this culture.

So, in order to be faithful to the unchanging, ever-present Jesus Christ and to the mission given it by Jesus Christ, the church must attend carefully and persistently to its circumstances. We live in a time of tremendous change and uncertainty. In such a time, the church has many opportunities for revitalized witness to the gospel. New ways of living out the gospel arise, and people who thought they had the church and the gospel figured out and written off may have to reconsider its relevance and truth. At the same time, the church's faithfulness to the gospel must be vigorously guarded. As circumstances change, new threats to the truth of the gospel may arise. For example, with religious freedom in Russia and the republics of the former Soviet Union, the church has tremendous opportunities to present the gospel to spiritually hungry people. At the same time, however, the church in those states has had to contend with the rise of religious cults—a problem that did not exist in the U.S.S.R. and one which the church is ill-prepared to meet.

Since changing circumstances bring new threats, the church must continually discern the characteristics of the particular culture within which it is called to faithfulness. This is true of the church in all times and places. The concern of this study will be the faithfulness of the church in Western culture.

One of the most powerful and far-reaching analyses of Western culture is Alasdair MacIntyre's *After Virtue*.[8] Although MacIntyre's later work grows beyond *After Virtue* in ways that we will consider below, *After Virtue* remains MacIntyre's seminal work and his most incisive analysis of Western culture. In this book, MacIntyre traces the history of Western moral traditions and argues that this history has brought us to a critical time in our culture. Although focused on ethical theory, MacIntyre's account incorporates a compact and incisive analysis of the whole of our society. We are faced, he says, with two paths, which we will explore in the following chapters. We may follow Nietzsche down the path that views morality as simply an expression of emotional preference and social relationships as an arena for the exercise of power. Or we may follow Aristotle down the path that leads to community rooted in the narrative of a tradition and embodied in certain virtues and practices.

MacIntyre's analysis provides some powerful lessons for the church's faithfulness. However, since MacIntyre's "tradition" in this analysis is more Aristotelian than Christian, we will have to make some adjustments as we follow his analysis. Following the writing of *After Virtue*, MacIntyre returned to the church, and his later works, *Whose Justice? Which Rationality?* and *Three Rival Versions of Moral Enquiry*, show the dominance of the Augustinian-Thomistic tradition in his thought. However, these later works do not display the same incisive analysis of Western culture found in the earlier work and even the turn to Christianity in them is incomplete.[9]

---

8. MacIntyre, *After Virtue* (1981; 2nd ed., 1984; 3rd ed., 2007). Refer-ences to this book will be made to the second edition. Since my concern here is to draw on MacIntyre's work for the sake of the church's faithfulness of the gospel, I will seldom engage the secondary arguments about MacIntyre's work. For that discussion and further references see the works by Horton and Mendus and Stout in the Bibliography.

9. See the criticisms in Milbank, *Theology*, 326–79; and Hauerwas and Pinches, *Christians*.

So even though we will have to make some adjustments along the way, *After Virtue* is the text from which we will draw several lessons for the church to live and witness faithfully. The first lesson is the need to attend to our history. Under the influence of modernity, the church has tended to be ahistorical. By telling the story of Western moral traditions, MacIntyre shows us that history constitutes an argument and determines the range of possibilities open to us. Therefore, in the first chapter I tell briefly the history of the church in relation to Western culture as that history determines how the church is to live and witness faithfully today. Given this history, we need new monastic communities that will live their lives before the watching world in such a way that our history as a church will be acknowledged in confession and repentance. Such confession and repentance requires an intentionally disciplined way of life that makes such practices integral expressions of life together with God and one another, not a marketing program or public relations ploy.

In the second chapter, I pursue MacIntyre's suggestion that we live in a fragmented world rather than a pluralistic world. I show the differences between fragmentation and pluralism and its significance for Christian mission. In the third chapter, I summarize MacIntyre's story of the mainstream of morality in Western culture and show how the church has compromised its faithfulness by accommodating to that mainstream and how many current conceptions of the mission of the church continue that mistake. In a new fourth chapter, I consider the Nietzschean reality and potentiality in our world as a powerful danger to living faithfully in a fragmented world. In the fifth chapter, I summarize MacIntyre's story of the minority, Aristotelian tradition in Western culture. I replace his account with one rooted in the gospel of Jesus Christ and the Christian community. In each of these chapters I show how MacIntyre's hope for a new monasticism responds to these analyses.

In the sixth chapter, I draw on the preceding chapters to develop MacIntyre's hope for a "new monasticism" in order to consider what forms the life of the church must take in order to sustain faithful witness in contemporary culture. In conclusion, I summarize my argument and identify some areas for further thought and action in response to all that has developed since the first edition of this book. I am especially concerned here to indicate briefly a theology for a new monasticism after modernity and post-Christendom.

The "Preface to the Series" in which the first edition of this book was published states that the series "(1) examines modern/postmodern culture from a missional point of view; (2) develops the theological agenda that the church in modern culture must address in order to recover its own integrity; and (3) tests fresh conceptualizations of the nature and mission of the church as it engages modern culture." Those are precisely the aims that this book seeks to advance through a very specific analysis of the threats to and possibilities for living faithfully in a fragmented world. As the years have passed since the first edition of the book, it is also clear that we are living in an increasingly postmodern culture. Part of the work of this new edition is to address the shift from modernity to postmodernity and the cultural overlap of the two. The flourishing of a new monastic movement indicates something about the rightness of the cultural analysis offered here and the guidance of the Holy Spirit in new monastic communities as one place to live in faithfulness to Jesus Christ.

ONE

Living with Our History

One of the most important lessons that the church can learn from *After Virtue* is implicit in the structure and approach of the book. In that book, MacIntyre narrates the history of two ethical theories, one springing from the Enlightenment, the other from Aristotle. For MacIntyre, telling these stories constitutes an argument about morality. Note that the story is not just an illustration of an argument or an example to aid understanding. The story *is* the argument.

In later chapters, we will consider the force of MacIntyre's argument for some form of the Aristotelian tradition. What concerns us here is not which tradition MacIntyre commends or whether he is right to commend it; rather, what concerns us is the form of MacIntyre's argument. For him, the confrontation between these two traditions can only be adjudicated by attending to their histories. These traditions are not two disembodied arguments whose strengths and weaknesses can be captured in a list and then compared. The very identification of them as "traditions" means that they have a history. MacIntyre teaches us that attending to that history— telling the stories of these traditions—itself constitutes an argument that may or may not commend a particular tradition.

Like these traditions, the church also has a history. Often, we study this history and tell it for seemingly trivial reasons—just to "know more" or to "add to our knowledge." So, we may memorize dates and names to impress our friends. Sometimes, we will study the history in order to understand Christian doctrine better. We may, for example, give considerable attention to the early church councils, where we worked out the central convictions of the church on the two natures of Jesus Christ and the doctrine of the Trinity. At times, we may give a lot of attention to periods when the church's history overlaps significantly with other historical concerns, such as the impact of revivalism on American culture. But, with a few notable exceptions, we have done very little to tell the history of the church as an argument for Christian faith.[1]

When I wrote the first edition of *Living Faithfully*, the church's history was already a problem in Western culture—the Crusades, witchcraft trials, support for slavery, and more were perceived by the culture as arguments against the truth of Christianity and the "good news of Jesus Christ." Since that first edition, the situation has gotten worse. The larger cultural mood may be well-captured by Dan Kimball's *They Like Jesus but Not the Church*.[2]

Today, the history of the church is perceived by many as one of the strongest arguments against belief in the good news of Jesus Christ. Even among those who "like Jesus" the approach to him is to pick what you like from his teaching and way of life and leave behind everything you don't like. A part of this practice includes choosing as your friends on this journey those with whom you are in general agreement. Even those who seek some new form of "church" often presume that it will exclude those who have been loyal to older forms of church.

In this context, new monastic communities are important in two ways. First, new monastic communities can offer a witness to the truth of the gospel by embracing the history of the church in confession and repentance. To engage in these practices, a community needs a life disciplined by the gospel and a deeply shared communal life. This does not mean that new monastic communities are closer to perfection that other "forms" of church. Indeed, the life of older and newer monastic communities is marked by conflict, sometimes very deep conflict. But what monastic communities have is a shared life, an intentionality, and a process that enables them to bear witness to the gospel in the ways that they engage in reconciliation with the history of the church, those alienated by its history, and their own community.

Second, new monastic communities embrace the history of the church in their "humble submission to Christ's body, the church," (Mark 5) and in their "hospitality to the stranger" (Mark 3). These marks of new

---

1. See, for example, Marsden, *Soul*, and van Braght, *Bloody Theater*.
2. Kimball, *They Like Jesus*.

monasticism commit its communities to the history of the church and to other forms of church that may be as likely to be strangers as anyone from outside the church.

Therefore, for these reasons, and others that we will encounter along the way, new monastic communities are crucial to the lesson that the church must learn to live with our history as an argument.

History-as-Argument

There are many reasons for our neglect of history-as-argument. Two are particularly important. First, we have tended to think of arguments on a model that was given to us by philosophy. On this model—there are others, but this one has predominated—arguments are constructed syllogistically; they are disembodied, ahistorical arguments for disembodied, ahistorical people. People have no history that influences their reason; positions likewise have no history that enters into an argument. One of MacIntyre's primary aims is to expose the failure of this presupposition, what in ethical theory he calls "the failure of the Enlightenment project." MacIntyre exposes this failure, not through a syllogistic argument, but by telling the history of the Enlightenment project so that we see its regrettable results. By narrating the failure of this project in moral terms, MacIntyre exposes the failure of the presupposition underlying ahistorical, disembodied arguments. From MacIntyre, the church should start learning how to tell its story as an argument for its witness to the Gospel.

The second reason that the church has neglected the notion of history-as-argument is a fear that our history would be an argument against rather than for the Gospel. Certainly there are grounds for this fear. The church has often sinned, and sinned greatly, against God and humanity in the name of the Gospel. But our fear is misplaced for several reasons. First, it mistakenly confuses the church and the Gospel. The Gospel is not just a message; it is the reality of God's redeeming activity through Jesus Christ.[3] The church is a human community called into existence by God and sustained by God as a witness to the Gospel, but the church is not the Gospel. The history of the church is the story of how far the church is from the Gospel, but it is also the history of how God uses the church to witness to God's redemption of creation. When the church is

3. I will occasionally use "the kingdom" as a shorthand image for this ever-present reality of the Gospel. For further development and defense of this notion, see Wilson, *Theology*, chapter 3.

unfaithful, God still makes the church a witness to the kingdom by God's judgment: "Judgment begins with the household of God" (1 Peter 4:17). Moreover, the history of the church's failures is the history of the church's recognition of its distance from the Gospel of Jesus Christ. That is, even the failures of the church may witness to the Gospel when those failures are recognized and properly confessed. Of course, we must be careful not to turn this into an argument for more sin in the church, as Paul imagines his interlocutors doing in Romans 6. Nevertheless, the point remains: the church is not the Gospel, so we must become more adept at telling the story of the church and the Gospel so that we witness to the Gospel.

Second, our fear of our history disembodies our faith. At the same time that we avoid the church's history we also avoid the history of the Gospel at work in this world. This double neglect disembodies the Gospel of Jesus Christ and renders it unreal in the world. One of the reasons that there is such a gap between most formal theology and the life of the church is that formal theology disembodies the Gospel. Real people and real lives have a history. We are not merely intellects processing logical arguments; we are human beings seeking a way of life. Week after week, preachers and other believers labor mightily to overcome this neglect and to embody the faith without significant help from theology. Now, there is certainly a place for formal theology. Indeed, this book is mostly an example of what I am criticizing. My plea is that we recognize the limitations of this approach and give more attention to history-as-argument.

If we do not attend to our history, in addition to confusing the Gospel and the church and disembodying the Gospel, we will become victims of our past. If we do not attend to our history, then the forces that have shaped us and brought us to this point will determine our fate. They become so familiar and comfortable that they become the very air that we breathe. As a consequence, we do not recognize the betrayals of the Gospel that have taken place, and we do not identify the distance between the Gospel and the church. In God's love for this world, God has never allowed the church to be completely faithless. God's judgment purifies and a remnant always remains as faithful witnesses. In these instances, the church's fear of its history results in a failure to recognize and confess our sin, and leads us into God's judgment so that we might be purified.

If we do not attend to our history, others also become victims of our past. The church has continually mistaken its judgment for God's will. History is replete with peoples who have been victimized by the church's mistaken judgments. As we continually deny these mistakes or suppress our memory of them, the church is bound to move on to other oppressive mistakes. We need continually to tell our story as confession of our unfaithfulness, so that the world may see beyond the church to the Gospel and so that we may all maintain a healthy suspicion of the church's confident pronouncements of God's will. In such a way, the church will be less likely to victimize others.

Often, the church denies its history in order to protect its existence. If we admit our past and its mistakes, that seems very much like an admission that the church has no necessary claim on existence. But that reasoning is contrary to the Gospel. In the Gospel, the church knows that we have been *given* everything necessary to life and salvation in Jesus Christ. In Jesus Christ, God has claimed this world for redemption: the church witnesses to that redemption, it has no need to claim this world for itself. The church's only reason for existence is as a witness to the Gospel of Jesus Christ. Therefore, the church is free to tell its story as confession, and in so doing free itself to witness to the kingdom.

In addition to denying our past, another mistake we can make is glorifying our past. In other words, rather than coping with the failures of the past by denying that we have a history, we may cope with the failures of the past by glorifying our successes and ignoring our failures.[4] Instead of a blanket denial of the past, we indulge in a selective denial. This is a serious temptation in Western culture, most especially in the United States, where the church can claim considerable influence on our culture. Looking back, we can glorify the past and lament the loss of the good old days when Christians were the majority or society at least accepted Christian values. Having made this step, we may then conclude that the mission of the church is to reassert this dominance in society.

This approach is easily identifiable today in much of the political action pursued in the name of Christianity. The church in the U.S., more than in any other nation marked by Western culture, looks to the past as a glorious time of Christian rule to which we must return if we are to turn away God's wrath. Two arguments stand against this approach. First, it

---

4. I do not have in mind here a similar-appearing approach that seeks to identify a thin thread of faithfulness in the history of the church. That approach is commendable as long as it does not confuse this "faithful remnant" with the kingdom or with the "only true believers." I will return to this later in the chapter.

represents the error of "Constantinianism."[5] Where denying our past may be a result of confusing the kingdom and the church, glorifying our past is often the result of confusing the kingdom and society. Since the conversion of the Emperor Constantine to Christianity and the subsequent rise of Christianity as the dominant religion of the empire in the early decades of the fourth century, the church has continually fallen into the error of thinking that the mission of the church was not to make disciples of Jesus Christ among all nations, but to rule the world by exercising power through political structures. According to this way of thinking, the mission of the church in the modern world is, first, to gain control of the political processes so that the laws of the land reflect Christian values and, second, to form church members into good citizens who will sustain the political life of the nation. In this way, our glorious Christian past will be revived for today.

This Constantinian understanding of the mission of the church may be born of a very commendable conviction that the church and the kingdom are embodied, visible realities today, but it ends up mistaking a human creation—the empire, the nation—for God's kingdom. When this happens, the existence of the kingdom and the church are thought to depend upon a particular state of affairs, such as a political system, a growing economy, a particular social structure, or the rule of a particular person. If we have confused the kingdom and a particular state of affairs, when that state of affairs changes, we become anxious about the existence of the kingdom and the church. We then mistakenly think that the mission of the church is to bring about, or help bring about, a return to the state of affairs upon which the kingdom depends.

Much of what passes for Christian mission today is motivated by precisely this way of thinking: the church actively promotes a return to some past state of affairs so that the kingdom may once again be present—so that God may once again "bless America." At this point, however, we have badly muddled the work of the Gospel and the relationship between the church, the world, and the kingdom. Certainly, the good news of Jesus Christ reveals God's work in this world. That work is not just a hoped-for future, it is a present reality. That reality is not just an interior state of being in the believer, it is a way of living out our social relationships. But that reality is not captive to some particular culture. The Gospel has been

---

5. For a fuller critique of "Constantinianism," see Yoder, *Priestly Kingdom*; Hauerwas and Willimon, *Resident Aliens*; and Hauerwas, *After Christendom*.

powerfully at work throughout many cultures, in all kinds of political systems, economic circumstances, encompassing many different rulers, nations, and languages. Nor is the reality of the Gospel captive to the past. It is presently at work in powerful ways that, by the grace of the Holy Spirit, we may discern throughout our world.

The temptation to glorify our past because of a "Constantinian" confusion of the kingdom and society disables that discernment and leads to a betrayal of the mission of the church. In such a situation, our task is to learn from the past how to disentangle our vision of church, world, and Gospel so that we can see the Gospel at work today.

In addition to confusing the kingdom and society, when the church glorifies our history we also mistake the character of the kingdom. The Gospel does reveal the glory of the kingdom of God in Jesus Christ, but it is the same glory that Jesus Christ revealed, the glory of servanthood: "Whoever would be great among you must become the least and the servant of all, for the Son of Man came not to be served but to serve and to give his life as a ransom for many" (Mark 10:45). This kind of glory is not the glory that is sought by those who confuse the kingdom and society. Just as Jesus Christ came as a servant, so also the church fulfills its mission to witness to this Gospel by serving. Those who glorify the past seek a return to the past by imposing the rule of the church on society. But the mission of the church is not to impose the Gospel or some state of affairs on the world in order to bring the kingdom. Rather, the church is called to witness to the Gospel. The Gospel is a gift, not an imposition, and the church's faithfulness to itl is measured in part by its unwillingness to impose its rule upon society.

Of course, to some this may sound like a recommendation for a weak church that can be manipulated by society. In fact, however, the opposite is the case. As I will later argue in detail in chapters 5 and 6, for the church to live and witness faithfully in our world, the church must be a highly disciplined, courageous community. It is the church that willingly adopts the power of the world that does not need discipline or courage—until it is brought face to face with God's judgment.

Finally, we must note that when the church succumbs to the temptation to glorify the past, it usually does so by narrowing its view of the kingdom to one particular state of affairs. When this happens, the work of the Gospel becomes restricted—often to one class, one race, sometimes even one sex, as the primary participants in the Gospel. That is, the glorification of the past usually identifies one particular tradition, time or place as *the* moment of faithfulness. This has the effect of excluding other people, times, and places from the possibility of faithfulness. This narrowing of the kingdom, then, betrays the commission to make disciples of *all peoples*.

THE CHURCH'S HISTORY IN WESTERN CULTURE

MacIntyre teaches us that living faithfully in this world means that the church must live with its history, neither denying that history nor glorifying it. For the purposes of this book, the history that will concern us is the history of the church in Western culture, that is, in European civilizations, particularly since the Enlightenment.[6] Indeed, "living with our history" means that the church must live with the effects of its influence on our culture. After Constantine, that is, after Christianity became the favored religion of the Empire, the church became the most powerful force in Western society. Political structures, educational institutions, social forms, and the theories that sustained them may all be traced to the influence of the church. That these institutions, forms, and theories took different and often conflicting shape does not change the fact that the power and language of the church was claimed by all of them. When rebellion and revolution were preached, they too came to us determined by the forms and languages of the church.

In European civilization, intellectual, political, and cultural history and practices can only be understood in relation to the history of the church. Given this, the history of the church becomes a terribly tangled web and a fearful burden. The church can be implicated in the worst events of our past: the medieval church and the Crusades, the German Church Movement and National Socialism, the American church and slavery, the Dutch Reformed Church and apartheid, and the list could go on. No matter how controversial and complex the church's involvement is, or how powerfully some in the church resisted these movements, it is still true that the church has been a dominant force in Western culture.

The dominance of the church in the history of our culture becomes particularly problematic as we move into a time when that dominance is

---

6. Although it is not the focus of this book, I should note that due to missionary activity and cultural expansion of the West, the history of the Western church includes the history of its impact on other cultures.

only a memory. Although we live in a culture that has been largely shaped by the influence of the church and by reactions to the church, other forces now dominate our culture. In the following two chapters we will look more closely at this situation. For now, I want to explore some ways in which this situation provides some unique threats and opportunities for the church to live faithfully and witness the Gospel of Jesus Christ.

As the church increasingly recognizes its minority status in Western culture, one obvious response will be to attempt to regain dominance in our culture. Tied into this strategy is the Constantinian presumption criticized above. It is in error both theologically and historically.[7] The better response is to ask ourselves this question:

> What must the church do in order to live and witness faithfully as
> a minority in a culture where we were once the majority?

This is the question that brings into focus the history of the church in Western culture and how we today are to live with our history.

There are two sources of instruction that are of limited help to us. They are helpful because they point us to other times and places when the church has been in a minority situation. They are limited because in neither instance did the minority church have to come to terms with a history of dominance. One source of guidance is the early church. Certainly, for the first three hundred years of its life, the church was a persecuted minority. Although sometimes admired, Christians had little or no social and political status *as Christians*. As Christians, they were also vulnerable legally and economically. Some who became Christians had already achieved some social, economic, and political power, but by becoming Christians they risked losing what they had gained. So, in the early history of the church, the church existed as a minority in a larger culture that was frequently hostile. Moreover, the early church witnessed to the Gospel in the midst of many competing claims to truth. The Mediterranean world of the early centuries was filled with a plethora of religions and gods to believe in.

These two characteristics of the early church—its the minority status and the diversity of beliefs in the culture around it—reflect the conditions faced by the church in Western culture today. We may learn from the

---

7. I do not make an argument for this assertion here. One of the main purposes of this book is to make an extended argument for this assertion and for a more appropriate response to our situation that will enable the church to live faithfully.

early church some lessons for how to live faithfully today, but we will also discover some limits to what we can learn from them. John Howard Yoder points out a number of lessons to learn from the early church about sustaining belief in the Lordship of Jesus Christ even though his followers are not mighty or numerous by the world's standards; about using language from the culture to communicate the Gospel of Jesus Christ; about how to witness to those in power; and other lessons.[8] But in this essay what Yoder does not clearly identify are the effects of the church's past on our present culture.

The early church did not have to live with the history of its having shaped the Mediterranean culture. So, for example, where the early church knew that it was encountering an alien, resistant, even hostile culture, the contemporary church in the West tends to think of the culture as benign, if not friendly, toward the Gospel. Where the early church knew that its message was new and strange, the contemporary church presents its message as familiar and comfortable. Where the early church sought to make its message understood, the contemporary church assumes that it is understood and seeks to persuade its hearers to accept what they understand. In each of these instances—and in many others—we have something to learn from the early church.

The contemporary church, however, faces some challenges not faced by the early church, because, as already noted, the early church did not have a history with which it had to live. For example, the early church did not have to answer for the way that its life had been intertwined with injustice, such as the church's support for slavery and segregation in the American South and apartheid in South Africa. Nor did the early church have a legacy of anti-Semitism to confess. Nor did the early church have a history of visible support for unjust and immoral rulers. All of this history has an effect on how we are to live faithfully today, and the practices of the early church gives us limited guidance here.

Moreover, as we will see in the next chapter, the contemporary church encounters a lot of apparently "Christian" words, concepts, and practices in our culture that are left over from the church's impact on that culture. These words, concepts, and practices may seem to convey the Gospel, but in the end they betray it because they have lost their rooting in the Gospel.

8. Yoder, *Priestly Kingdom*, chapter 1.

The early church did not face this danger, because they knew that the culture they were encountering was not Christian. We can learn from the early church what it means to take language captive for the Gospel, but we face a special danger, due to the lingering effects of the church on our culture.

In addition to the early church, we may also find some limited guidance from the experience of Western missionaries and churches in countries outside European civilization. Of course, due to missionary activity and the expansion of Western political and economic power aided by technology, European civilization has had a global impact. For these reasons the Western church has much to learn from churches in these other countries.[9] "Third World" churches are producing a number of theologians and church leaders who are addressing the Western church with challenging questions. These observers often see us more clearly than we see ourselves. They challenge our complicity with Western political and economic powers, and expose our cultural blindness.

Likewise, missiologists and other Westerners who have been shaped by non-Western churches have some profound lessons to teach us. Two of those missiologists are William Dyrness and Lesslie Newbigin. In *How Does America Hear the Gospel?* Dryness, who taught in the Philippines for many years, teaches us what many other missionaries have been saying, that we in the West need to look at our culture from a missionary perspective.[10] For many decades we have been critically attentive to other cultures as we have sought to present the Gospel, but we have not been critically attentive to our own culture. It has been as natural to us as the air we breathe, and, as a result, we have not thought of our own culture as a threat to our faithfulness or as an object of careful analysis. Now, through the kind of work that Dyrness represents, we are learning to approach our own culture as missionaries. Newbigin, who served several decades in South India, including nearly twenty years as a bishop of the Church of South India, "retired" to England in 1974. In retirement, he has turned his attention to the spiritual plight of the West. He has written a series of

9. I despair of finding a suitable term for what I am trying to describe. By "Western church" I mean those churches located in countries dominated by Western culture, mainly in Europe and North America, though New Zealand and Australia may be included. Additionally, many churches outside of these geographical boundaries may be so "Western" as to be indistinguishable from the churches to which I refer.

10. Dryness, *How Does America.*

books that analyze Western culture from a missionary perspective.[11] As a Westerner who has spent much of his life ministering in India, Newbigin offers some powerful analyses and insights. He is particularly sensitive to the effects of the Enlightenment on Western culture and to the challenge it represents for communicating the Gospel.

Although Dyrness and Newbigin bring missionary insights from the Third World that we will draw on in the following chapters, they do not attend to the life of the church in the history of Western culture as closely as we will. They concentrate instead on the interaction of the Gospel and culture, rather than the church and culture. As a result, neither one develops a full and clear account of the church's relationship to Western culture or of the changing status of the church and its significance for the church's mission.

THE FIRST LESSON

How are we to live faithfully as the church in our culture? The first lesson that MacIntyre teaches us is that in order to live faithfully, the church must learn to live with its history. Learning to live with our history means learning to distinguish among the church, the kingdom, and the world as we tell our story. If we learn to make these distinctions, then we will neither deny nor glorify the history of the church. Instead we will be able to bear witness to the Gospel in the midst of the church's faithfulness and unfaithfulness. By attending to our history, we will also learn to think like missionaries about our own culture. If we learn to think about our own history and culture in this way, then we will be able to discern the threats to and possibilities for living faithfully in the midst of our fragmented world.

New monastic communities live out this lesson by sharing their lives—their embodied lives—with one another in community. They live in close proximity to one another and share meals together as a community and as a practice of hospitality with those who are not members. They share their possessions with one another in ways discerned and agreed to by the community. They make their life visible to one another and to the world, so they do not appeal to some "invisible church" as an explanation for unfaithfulness. Rather, they have the courage, humility, and discipline to confess their sin and receive God's discipline and forgiveness.

11. Newbigin, *Foolishness; Pluralist Society; Truth to Tell.*

TWO

Fragmented Worlds

MacIntyre begins *After Virtue* with "a disquieting suggestion" that we live in a fragmented world.[1] He draws out the implications of this suggestion through the following scenario:

> Imagine that the natural sciences were to suffer the effects of a catastrophe. A series of environmental disasters are blamed by the general public on the scientists. Widespread riots occur, laboratories are burnt down, physicists are lynched, books and instruments are destroyed. Finally, a Know-Nothing political movement takes power and successfully abolishes science teaching in schools and universities, imprisoning and executing the remaining scientists. Later still there is a reaction against this destructive movement and enlightened people seek to revive science, although they have largely forgotten what it was. But all they possess are fragments; a knowledge of experiments detached from any knowledge of the theoretical context which gave them significance; parts of theories unrelated either to the other bits and pieces of theory which they possess or to experiment; instruments whose use has been forgotten; half-chapters from books, single pages from articles, not always fully legible because torn and charred. None the less all these fragments are reembodied in a set of practices which go under the revived names of physics, chemistry, and biology. Adults argue with each other about the respective merits of relativity

---

1. MacIntyre's "disquieting suggestion" is presented at the beginning of his work as a hypothesis that depends for its force upon the extensive analysis that follows. I have chosen to follow MacIntyre's order of presentation here. If the reader is less than persuaded by this suggestion, I urge patience as the argument develops.

theory, evolutionary theory, and phlogiston theory, although they possess only a very partial knowledge of each. Children learn by heart the surviving portions of the periodic table and recite as incantations some of the theorems of Euclid. Nobody, or almost nobody, realises that what they are doing is not natural science in any proper sense at all. For everything that they do and say conforms to certain canons of consistency and coherence and those contexts which would be needed to understand what they are doing have been lost, perhaps irretrievably.[2]

Building on this imaginary scenario, MacIntyre argues that

in the actual world which we inhabit the language of morality is in the same state of grave disorder as the language of natural science in the world which I described. What we possess, if this view is true, are the fragments of a conceptual scheme, parts of which now lack those contexts from which their significance derived. We possess indeed simulacra of morality, we continue to use many of the key expressions. But we have—very largely, if not entirely—lost our comprehension, both theoretical and practical, of morality.[3]

The importance of this claim and MacIntyre's supporting arguments cannot be overstated, even though we might want to make some adjustments.[4] His narrative displays the ways in which our culture lost the conceptual scheme(s) that gave meaning to our morality and thus ended up with only fragments. In this chapter I will describe this fragmentation and show how the church participates in it. I will also show how the fragmented church often mistakes our disordered language for well-ordered language and has only a simulacrum of Christian mission.

MacIntyre argues that we live in a world in which morality exists only in fragments. These fragments give us only an appearance of morality, not its reality. What the church must learn from this is that our understanding of the gospel, our witness, and our discipleship are also deeply fragmented. We have only a semblance of the gospel, not its reality, at work in our life together. Consequently, "Christians" are deeply vulnerable to ideologies that will use the language of Christianity and make appeals to the gospel in order to co-opt the church for programs

2. MacIntyre, *After Virtue*, 1.

3. Ibid., 2.

4. Horton and Mendus, *After MacIntyre*; Milbank, *Theology*; below, chapter 5.

and purposes that are contrary to the gospel. We have no firm center in the gospel but are preoccupied with and distracted by peripheral matters that exploit our fragmentation.

In these circumstances, we have much work to do to overcome our fragmentation and recover a coherent, more holistic practice of the gospel. To do this will require hard, persistent work by communities rooted in a provisional understanding of this fragmentation. This understanding must be provisional because the very character of fragmentation means that those whose lives are fragmented only perceive that fragmentation indirectly, through unease or an initially inchoate sense that something may not be quite right.

With this provisional understanding of our fragmentation, these communities will then set for themselves an intentional commitment to a way of life that seeks greater coherence and congruence in their life of discipleship. This again will require hard work, a commitment to stable relationships over a long period of time, and a willingness to share life together (commune) in such a way that this shared life is centered in Christ so that the fragments are pulled together by the gravitational pull of this center. In all of this, these communities must acknowledge and celebrate the grace of God as a power that reveals and heals the fragmentation of our lives.

This is a critically important lesson to be learned from MacIntyre: that we live in a fragmented world not a pluralistic world. If we lived in a pluralistic world with relatively intact multiple communities, then the recovery of Christian faithfulness would entail the strengthening and maturing of those communities. We would simply need to work with the social arrangements that we currently have to direct them properly. Indeed, many of the books written today for the church assume just this situation. The church as we have it is intact and just needs some reorganizing and reprogramming, perhaps better leadership.

If we live in a fragmented world, then we do not have relatively intact communities of discipleship in the church. Instead, we have fragments of discipleship in fragments of community. But we persist in the belief (and often the self-deception) that we have a good understanding of discipleship and good communities. MacIntyre's argument for fragmentation over pluralism as the proper interpretation of our circumstances means that we need new forms of community—new monastic communities— if we are going to recover an authentic discipleship in communities of disciples. After an analysis of MacIntyre's argument, we will see how his interpretation leads to the necessity of new monastic communities.

In other words, as we inchoately sense and vaguely see the fragmentation of the gospel in our lives, the recovery of wholeness in our understanding of the gospel and our life in Christ may be found in God's gracious calling of new monastic communities.

Pluralism is not the Problem

Before we can understand the significance of the fragmentation of our culture, we must examine a pervasive description of contemporary culture that seems very much like this concept of fragmentation, but which ultimately misleads us about the changes and challenges that the church faces today. One of the most popular ways of characterizing the challenge of the modern world to Christian mission is to say that we live in a "pluralistic world." This pluralism is supposed to be a particular challenge for a church that has lived in a monolithic world for so long and has not had to compete with other claims to truth. On the basis of this characterization, many have looked to the early church and to missionary situations in the Third World for guidance, as we saw in the previous chapter.

The second lesson that we learn from MacIntyre's *After Virtue* is that we live, not in a pluralistic world, but among fragmented worlds. As we will see, this characterization makes the challenge of our situation much deeper than pluralism. After we examine the more familiar description of pluralism and its limitations for describing our situation, we will consider how to meet the challenges of living faithfully among fragmented worlds.

"Pluralism," as I am using it here, describes a world of competing outlooks, traditions, or claims to truth. It pictures a culture made up of coherent, integral communities, traditions, or positions that can be clearly differentiated from one another. Although they disagree and may often be in conflict, where these disagreements are located and why they arise are generally clear to everyone. One's identity—as an individual or community—is clear, the convictions that constitute that identity are coherent, and the life that follows from those convictions is determined. When one of these communities breaks down, we can say how it has failed. So even though there are many competing communities, identities, or positions, pluralism describes a situation in which these competing outlooks are mostly coherent and clearly defined.

MacIntyre argues that characterizing our culture in terms of pluralism is misleading and obscures the real challenge that we face. In his analysis, Western culture is fragmented, not pluralistic. It is incoherent; our lives are lived piecemeal, not whole. The disagreements that we have are difficult to resolve because we cannot locate them within some coherent position or community. We do not live in a world filled with competing outlooks; we live in a world that has fallen apart.[5]

Although "pluralism" is often used to describe the new situation and challenges facing the church, it more nearly describes the world in which I grew up in the American Midwest and South in the 1950s and 1960s. We are used to thinking of American culture in the 1950s and early 1960s as monolithic. However, in those years, we were all acutely aware that we lived in a world of competing communities and traditions. The melting pot was full of unmeltable goods.

In order to make this claim clearer, let's consider the competition between two groups of Baptists. I grew up as the son of a pastor in the National Association of Free Will Baptists. Free Will Baptists number about 250,000 and are located primarily in the South and Midwest. Their theology is Arminian—it is possible to believe in Christ, then fall away from him. At the time I was growing up, Free Will Baptists were also separatist fundamentalists—many so-called Christians really are not Christians, and we should keep separate from them. We were very clear about the differences between us and other churches, even other Baptists. If we were told that someone was a Free Will Baptist, we could say clearly how that person would be different from a Southern Baptist. Southern Baptists believed that once you were saved, you could not lose your salvation, so they were not nearly so careful about Christian living as were Free Will Baptists. We were sure Southern Baptists really were "Christians who don't drink in front of each other." Southern Baptist women did not dress as modestly as Free Will Baptists—they used more make-up, wore more jewelry, and some wore trousers—and Southern Baptist men were not as trustworthy in business as Free Will Baptists.

---

5. This characterization must be slightly qualified, because we in the West are encountering coherent outlooks in various schools of Islam and Asian traditions of Buddhism and Hinduism. This is one reason why these are so attractive to Westerners and why they present a significant challenge to the Western church. As part of the fragmentation of Western culture, the Western church often finds itself impotent in the face of challenges from coherent alternatives.

As with these two close relatives, so also with other communities and traditions: if we knew which church a person belonged to, we could tell you about his or her life. Nazarenes, the Christian Church, the Presbyterians, the Methodists, the Catholics, and in larger cities, Jews, were part of our world. But it was a pluralistic world populated by coherent communities with clear boundaries.

Certainly, pluralism may be used to describe any number of situations. The most helpful use of the term identifies the kind of situation I have been describing, where competing communities and traditions represent relatively coherent, clearly distinguishable entities. Today, however, we are often drawn to this term because we live in a world with increasing options and with increasing differences between options. It is true that there are more options today: I did not grow up in a world where Hindus, Buddhists, and Moslems were my neighbors. So both the variety and differences are greater today. But to think that "pluralism" captures the real significance of the changes in our culture misconstrues the change and the challenge that it represents.

LIVING AMONG FRAGMENTS

In order to live faithfully today, we must recognize that we have not moved from a monolithic world into a pluralistic world; rather, we have moved from a time when our communities were relatively coherent and clear, to a time when our communities and traditions have become fragmented—incoherent and fuzzy. Certainly, some coherent communities still exist, but these are communities that for various reasons have not been a part of our cultural change. For example, the Amish, as well as Hasidic Jews, remain relatively coherent as communities because they have not participated in the larger cultural shifts. Recent Moslem immigrants have coherent communities because their participation in Western culture is relatively recent.[6] In contrast, communities like Free Will Baptists and Southern Baptists have fragmented so much that one can no longer be sure of properly identifying or describing a member of either tradition. (Of course, Free Will Baptists would want to say that you can still tell them from Presbyterians.)

6. This claim is independent of the question of whether people remain within a tradition. The tradition and community may remain coherent even if people decide to leave it. Since many Moslems have only recently immigrated, how their communities and traditions contend with fragmentation remains to be seen.

The church in the West is fragmented because its life has for so long been intertwined with the larger culture. As that culture has fragmented, so also has the church. MacIntyre's narrative of this fragmentation centers on morality. He shows that moral schemes that were previously coherent depended for their coherence upon a conceptual scheme that gave a description of (1) where humans are on a moral landscape, (2) where they should be, and (3) how to get from where they are to where they should be. In a lengthy and powerful analysis, MacIntyre shows how and why modern culture abandoned the second element of this scheme—any convictions about where humans should be—our *telos* (goal, purpose, end). Once any notion of *telos* is abandoned, we are left with "where humans are" and "what we should do." But "what we should do"—morality— makes no sense apart from a *telos*. So our moral language, practice, and concepts linger as fragments of a previously coherent account. As time goes on, these moral fragments appear arbitrary, mere exercises of power or expressions of emotion.[7]

FRAGMENTATION IN THE CHURCH

This same fragmentation has deeply affected the moral life of the church, but its effects are not limited to morality. The entire life of the church has been deeply affected by this fragmentation. If we cling to pluralism and neglect fragmentation as a description of our situation, we will become more vulnerable over time and will cease to live and witness faithfully. We will have the appearance of life and health, but it will only be simulacra of the church's calling.

We can guard against this happening by attending to two areas of the church's life that are radically challenged by this fragmentation. Our analysis will not be exhaustive; rather, it will be suggestive of the kinds of threats the church faces and possible ways of living faithfully. As we look at these areas of fragmentation in the life of the church, we will observe a number of interwoven complications. We will discover that when we lose the *telos*, or over-arching conceptual scheme that gives meaning to language and practice, then that language and practice becomes more easily assimilated to other purposes and other sources of meaning. We will also discover that fragmentation affects both the internal and external life of the church. That is, since the life of the church has been so

7. Kallenberg et al., *Virtues*, 7–29.

intertwined with the culture, the fragmentation of church and culture means that there are fragments of the church's influence present in the larger culture. The church may easily mistake these fragments as coherent understandings of the gospel, and, as a result, fall into serious miscommunication that is almost impossible to recognize and untangle. Finally, as we explore this fragmentation, we will discover that individuals live fragmented lives. One moment their language and practice is ordered to one community and tradition, the next moment, another community and tradition determines their language and practice. Once again, this kind of incoherence is very difficult to identify and untangle, but with MacIntyre's help we may begin to discern some of this incoherence.

One area of the life of the church that is deeply affected by fragmentation is our worship. As the Westminster Catechism states, "the chief end of [humanity] is to glorify God and enjoy [God] forever." When this *telos* is lost and (pseudo)worship ensues, then our practice of worship may appear healthy while actually being ordered by the wrong end.

Such a situation is not new; Isaiah describes just such circumstances:

> Hear the word of the LORD,
> you rulers of Sodom!
> Listen to the teaching of our God,
> you people of Gomorrah!
>
> What to me is the multitude of your sacrifices?
> says the LORD;
> I have had enough of burnt offerings of rams
> and the fat of fed beasts;
> I do not delight in the blood of bulls, or of lambs, or of goats.
>
> When you come to appear before me,
> who asked this from your hand?
>
> Trample my courts no more;
> bringing offerings is futile;
> incense is an abomination to me.
> New moon and sabbath and calling of convocation—
> I cannot endure solemn assemblies with iniquity.
>
> Your new moons and your appointed festivals my soul hates;
> they have become a burden to me,
> I am weary of bearing them.
>
> When you stretch out your hands,
> I will hide my eyes from you;
> even though you make many prayers,

I will not listen;
your hands are full of blood.

Wash yourselves; make yourselves clean;
remove the evil of your doings from before my eyes;
cease to do evil;
learn to do good;
seek justice,
rescue the oppressed,
defend the orphan,
plead for the widow. (Isaiah 1:10–17, NRSV)

Here, Isaiah describes a community that clearly engages enthusiastically in worship. They bring their best animals as sacrifices and they have even added new times of worship. But in spite of this care and enthusiasm, the community is under the threat of God's judgment, because they have forgotten the purpose of worship. Their lives are so fragmented that they can "worship" the God of justice, the God of the oppressed, but not live out that conviction in the rest of their lives. Apparently, outside of formal worship, their lives were ordered by other ends—prosperity, security, pleasure.

Like these ancient Israelites, the people of God in the Western church have forgotten that the purpose of worship is to teach us to glorify God and enjoy God forever in the whole of our lives. Since our practice of worship has been severed from this end, and since our own lives are governed by competing, incompatible ends, our "worship" becomes disordered, even when it appears orderly and enthusiastic. As a result of this disordering, we try to make worship serve other purposes. So, for example, if we accept another version of the human *telos*—that we are to be happy, well-adjusted people—then we expect worship to be a kind of mass therapy session that makes us feel better. Or, if we believe that the human *telos* is to be successful professionally, then we expect worship to be a kind of mass pep rally that energizes us for the week ahead. We can even distort the purpose of worship by believing that the human *telos* is a happy, healthy family. And so we expect that worship will be ordered to that end.

The difficulty here, of course, is that all of these seem like such admirable, faithful purposes—who wants to be maladjusted, unsuccessful, and unhappy? The mistake that we make is that these purposes disorder our worship; that is, they are proper consequences of worship rightly ordered to the purpose of glorifying God and enjoying God forever. Take, for instance, the quest for a happy, well-adjusted life. In connection with this quest, its defenders ask, "Should not worship make us feel better? We all have difficult, demanding lives. Shouldn't worship be a place of healing and encouragement?" Of course, worship should make us "feel better" and encourage us, but it properly does so when it is ordered to the right end. If we approach worship as a mass therapy session, then the effect of worship is to make us "feel better" and "encourage us" by changing our emotional state and our self-perception. However, the proper end of worship is to confront us with the vision of God and reorient our lives to this vision. If our worship is ordered by this end, then we will not merely feel better, we will be blessed, and our perception of the world, not just our perception of ourselves, will be changed. This vision and reorientation will change the way that we live in the world. But that change is possible only with the discernment, support, and admonition of others who live in close relationship with us beyond our time of worship together. If one or two hours of worship together each week is the whole of our life together, then the fragmentation of our lives will not be healed.

Worship will indeed make us feel better and encourage us; but when properly ordered, worship places these results within a coherent community and tradition, not a fragmented, incoherent life. Properly ordered worship will engage the whole of our lives. That is, properly ordered worship integrates all of life into a coherent whole so that what we confess and enact in communal worship extends over the rest of our lives. Since our culture and our lives are so fragmented, this demand for coherence appears strange and entails pain and struggle. But to live faithfully in a fragmented world requires just this kind of ordering in our worship.[8] And living faithfully requires that our lives be shared with others in intentional commitment to this reordering that heals our fragmentation.

Since this fragmentation and disordering of our worship is so subtle, one additional insight from MacIntyre may help us discern and correct our disorder. In MacIntyre's discussion of "practices," he distinguishes between "internal" and "external" goods.[9] "External" goods are precisely that—goods that may be acquired through some activity but which are themselves external to that activity. On the other hand, "internal" goods

8. I will further explore how to order our worship in chapter 5.

9. MacIntyre, *After Virtue*, 187–91. There is a great deal more than this to learn from MacIntyre's account of practices. We will return to this lesson in chapter 5.

are goods intrinsic to an activity—they cannot be truly conceived, experienced, or understood apart from a particular kind of activity. So, for example, someone may play basketball to achieve external goods, such as status, fame, a college scholarship, or a multimillion-dollar, professional contract. Although these goods are acquired through playing basketball, they really exist independently of basketball. Or one could play basketball in order to achieve goods internal to the game—participating in a team endeavor, the pleasure of physical exercise, the thrill of bodily movement ordered toward excellence. These goods cannot be conceived, experienced, or understood apart from the actual *practice* of playing basketball or some similar sport. To play basketball for internal goods makes basketball a practice.

This distinction between external and internal goods can help us discern the disorder of our worship when we ask ourselves to which of these our worship is ordered. Do we seek through our worship goods that are extrinsic to worship? Or do we seek goods intrinsic to worship, goods that cannot be conceived, experienced, or understood apart from worship? To achieve humanity's true end—to glorify and enjoy God—simply *is* to worship; one cannot conceive a way of glorifying and enjoying God apart from the practice of worship. So, if the things that we are seeking in and through worship can be conceived apart from worship, our worship is disordered. More strongly still, in biblical terms worship that is ordered toward some end other than glorifying and enjoying God is idolatry. In our fragmented world and lives, we need to attend carefully to our "order" of worship in order to live faithfully.

Another area of contemporary fragmentation that has a tremendous impact on the possibility of living faithfully is the continued presence in our culture of leftover Christian language and symbols. In our culture the cross has become a fragmented symbol, as the following story reveals.[10] Some years ago, a friend went into a jewelry store in the town where he lives, Santa Barbara, California. When the clerk asked if she could help him, he said, "Yes, I would like to look at some crosses." She replied, "Would you like to see ones with the little man on them, or ones without?"

Now, for many years in our culture the cross has been worn by people with no commitment to Jesus Christ and even by those who clearly

10. The cross is not merely a symbol; it is most importantly a historic event in the life of Jesus Christ that is our redemption. Nevertheless, today actual crosses are "fragmented symbols" in the sense that I am going to develop.

despise the way of Jesus. But still in those situations the cross was a coherent symbol; people could say what it stood for, even if it had no personal significance for them. In the clerk's reply, we have a perfect example of a fragmented symbol: for her, as for many others, there is no community and no larger conceptual scheme to give the cross meaning.

The fact that the cross and not, for instance, a hammer and sickle, is the symbol in question, indicates the confluence of the church's history in our culture and the present fragmentation of our culture. This fragmented symbol is a powerful warning of the difficulties faced by the church in its attempts to live faithfully. Since Christianity has such a long history of influence in Western culture, many of the words, symbols, concepts, and activities of our culture appear to have their origins and meaning bound up in the church's witness to Jesus Christ. However, since we live in fragmented worlds today, those words, symbols, concepts, and activities may be profoundly deceptive. Take, for example, the simple declaration of the good news, "Jesus Christ died on the cross for the forgiveness of sins." The words "Jesus Christ" are very common, more common perhaps outside the church than inside, but there they are simply words of profanity. As we have already seen, although the cross is pervasive in our culture, it is a fragmented symbol, or worse, a symbol of racist and sexist oppression. As L. Gregory Jones has recently shown, the notion of forgiveness is a deeply fragmented concept and practice in our culture; it has been captured by the therapeutic and eclipsed by violence.[11] Cornelius Plantinga has done the same for our understanding of sin.[12]

Without saying so explicitly or at length, these analyses point up some of the deeply fragmented areas of our lives and culture. For the church to live faithfully, we must recognize the dynamic of this fragmentation. As Isaiah's oracle and MacIntyre's parable point out, a fragmented world may be marked by the appearance of a lively faithfulness in language and practice. The church may appear to be using all the right words and engaging in all the right activities, but if the church and the culture are fragmented, then that appearance is profoundly deceptive.

THE SECOND LESSON

So, MacIntyre's second lesson for the church is that we live among fragments. In the midst of this fragmentation, we may appear to be doing

11. Jones, *Embodying*.
12. Plantinga, *Not the Way*.

many "Christian" things; but if our activity is not ordered to our proper end, then that activity is unfaithful. This unfaithfulness is greatly complicated by the very nature of our situation which makes it difficult for us to discern our unfaithfulness. In order to untangle these complications a bit further, we turn next, with MacIntyre's help, to the history that has led to our fragmentation.

One means by which God's grace comes to us in the midst of this fragmentation is the calling together of new monastic communities. The communities arise outside the structures and activities of the church that are deeply intertwined with our fragmented world. As I have done in this chapter, we need to continue to explore how the life of the church has become fragmented along with our culture. But we must do so to seek the healing of the church, not to assign blame. To the extent that we learn to live with our history as part of this fragmentation, the church also may learn something about the coherence of the gospel by confessing its sin, accepting God's forgiveness, and bearing witness to Christ in this restorative practice.

THREE

The Failure of the Enlightenment Project

As we saw in the previous chapter, we live today among fragmented worlds. The first half of *After Virtue* identifies the source of this fragmentation by narrating "the failure of the Enlightenment project." This project seeks a rational justification for morality that is independent of any particular convictions, especially theological convictions. At one level, it may be understood as an attempt to end the seventeenth- and eighteenth-century conflicts in Europe that were rooted in religious differences. At another level, the Enlightenment project of morality may be read as the rejection of the classical moral tradition. MacIntyre shows that today this project and its failure lie at the root of the problems that both occupy academic philosophers *and* afflict our everyday social life.[1]

The failure of this project results not only in the fragmentation of life that is so destructive and deadly, it also results in an understanding of morality that leads us eventually into an "emotivist" view of life. As we will see later in this chapter, emotivism regards moral statements and claims as mere expressions of emotion. When someone says that adultery is immoral or cannibalism is wrong, all they are doing is describing their emotional response to adultery or cannibalism. They are saying that they find adultery or cannibalism disgusting, but their statements cannot go beyond a mere expression of personal preference.

When this emotivist understanding of morality encompasses all of life, it becomes a particularly significant obstacle to living faithfully. If the convictions that guide our way of life are merely expressions of personal

1. MacIntyre, *After Virtue*, chapter 4.

preference, then what's true for you is not necessarily true for others. In this emotivist world, what is important is that each of us is free to choose our personal preferences for living. In this context, the only immoral acts are believing that there is only one way to life and restricting others' freedom to choose and live as they prefer.

In the wake of the failure of the Enlightenment project and the rise of emotivist morality, the development of new monastic communities is essential to the faithfulness of the church. These communities contribute to the faithfulness of the church in at least three ways. First, in the intentionality of their living they display an alternative to the Enlightenment project of morality. Secondly, in their living by a rule of life they refuse to allow the failure of the Enlightenment project to determine their way of life. Thirdly, in their commitment to one another they set aside personal preference as the great good of human existence. To see these contributions clearly, we must first examine the failure of the Enlightenment project and the resultant (im)moral context in which we live.

THE CULTURE'S "ENLIGHTENMENT PROJECT"

After narrating the history of successive attempts to achieve an independent rational justification for morality in the work of Hume (who sought justification in the passions), Diderot (desire), Kant (reason), and Kierkegaard (choice), MacIntyre argues that these attempts ultimately fail, not because they looked to the wrong sources for justifying morality, but because they had in common a particular way of characterizing the problem—in short, they were all seeking to achieve "the Enlightenment project." This project was bound to fail, MacIntyre argues, because it misconstrued the moral tradition that it had inherited.

According to MacIntyre, the moral tradition previous to the Enlightenment depended, as I briefly noted in the previous chapter, upon a three-fold structure: (1) humanity as we are, (2) humanity as we should be, (3) how we can get from where we are to where we should be.[2] The Enlightenment project abandoned any notion of "humanity as we should be," because any account of who we should be depends upon a view of the true end of humanity that is rooted in particular convictions—the very thing that the Enlightenment sought to avoid. So the Enlightenment

---

2. MacIntyre *After Virtue*, 54. See Kallenberg et al., *Virtues*, 12, figure 2, for a graphic presentation of MacIntyre's claim.

project abandoned this three-fold structure and attempted to justify morality apart from any particular view of what humanity could be if we
realized our true end. As a result, the Enlightenment left us with humanity as we are and moral instruction for how to get from where we are
to . . . ? Since the Enlightenment abandoned all accounts of where we
should be, it could give no description of the purpose of morality. Thus,
moral precepts lacked the structure that had given them meaning and
coherence. Consequently, MacIntyre argues, "the Enlightenment project
had to fail."[3] We still have some of the language and practices of morality,
but they exist only in fragments, apart from the overall structure which
gave them meaning. This fragmented morality appears to have no justification, since it has been deprived of the very convictions that give it
meaning. Increasingly, then, morality seems to be merely a set of (often
personal) preferences.

As a result of this history, our culture is largely shaped by emotivism—
"the doctrine that all evaluative judgments and more specifically all moral
judgments are *nothing but* expressions of preference, expressions of at-
titude or feeling, insofar as they are moral or evaluative in character."[4] In
such a culture

> moral judgments, being expressions of attitude or feeling, are nei-
> ther true nor false; and disagreement in moral judgment is not to
> be secured by any rational method, for there are none. It is to be
> secured, if at all, by producing certain non-rational effects on the
> emotions or attitudes of those who disagree with mine. We use
> moral judgments not only to express our own attitudes and feel-
> ings, but also precisely to produce such effects in others.[5]

If the church is to live faithfully in the context of an emotivist culture
marked by the failure of the Enlightenment project, then we must learn a
number of things from MacIntyre's account.

The Church's "Enlightenment Project"

In order to understand the impact of the Enlightenment project on the
life of the church, we must first attend to ways in which the church is implicated in the Enlightenment project to achieve an independent rational

3. MacIntyre, *After Virtue*, chapter 5.

4. Ibid., 11–12.

5. Ibid., 12.

justification for morality. Certainly, the moral tradition of the Western church, because of our involvement with our culture, has been deeply affected by the failure of the Enlightenment project. This was the concern of the previous chapter, where we saw how the fragmentation of morality poses a serious threat to faithful living.

Of equal significance as a threat to the life of the church is the fact that the church has carried on its own version of the Enlightenment project in relation, not to morality, but to the Gospel. That is, just as Western culture, in the Enlightenment project, sought an independent rational justification for morality, so also the Western church has sought independent rational justification for the Gospel. And just as the Enlightenment project to justify morality was bound to fail, for the same reasons the church's version of the Enlightenment project also had to fail.

The church's quest for an independent rational justification of the Gospel has taken a number of forms. It is clearly evident in our apologetics, where there has been considerable debate. It is also the main theme of Hans Frei's influential analyses of hermeneutics and modern theology.[6] Of greatest interest for us is the way that the church's Enlightenment project has marked our "evangelism."

In contrast to the studies of apologetics, rationality, and hermeneutics, the church's language about and practice of evangelism has received little analysis along these lines. In order to initiate some examination of this tendency in evangelism, rather than examine specific practices and programs of evangelism, I will here sketch some general characteristics of the church's Enlightenment project on evangelism.[7]

The overarching characteristic of this project is the church's attempt to commend the Gospel on grounds that have nothing to do with the Gospel itself. In this way, the church avoids any convictions particular to the Gospel or the church as the basis for justifying or commending the Gospel. Two things result from this attempt. First, as with MacIntyre's narrative of the Enlightenment project on morality, the church seeks various grounds for the Gospel. Commensurate with the attempts of Hume, Diderot, Kant, and Kierkegaard on behalf of morality, the church has had its thinkers who have sought to ground the Gospel in accounts of the passions, desires, reason, and choice. This has been true of both academic

---

6. Frei, *Eclipse*; *Types*; *Theology and Narrative*.
7. See Kallenberg, *Live to Tell*; Stone, *Evangelism*.

and popular theology. For example, Kant's attempt to ground morality in reason is accompanied by an attempt to ground religion "within the bounds of reason alone." Here an account of reason that is independent of the Gospel becomes the putative ground—and boundary—for religion. Likewise, Friedrich Schleiermacher's *On Religion: Speeches to its Cultured Despisers* may be read as an evangelistic presentation of the Gospel that seeks to commend the Gospel on the basis of the feeling of absolute dependence. Since Schleiermacher's account of the feeling of absolute dependence is developed without reference to the Gospel and does not depend upon the Gospel for its meaning, his account is an expression of the church's Enlightenment project.[8]

On a more popular level, we may often hear evangelistic presentations that commend the Gospel to its hearers on their terms, rather than seeking to present a coherent account of the Gospel's own faithfulness. For example, Robert Schuller's widely known attempt at a "new reformation" based on self-esteem fails, not because self-esteem is the wrong way to "translate" the Gospel for contemporary people, but because Schuller's account develops the notion of self-esteem separate from the structure of the Gospel, then makes our quest for self-esteem the ground for commending the Gospel.[9] In other words, the fundamental problem with Schuller's appeal is not the notion of self-esteem itself, but the structure to which Schuller appeals for the meaning of self-esteem. Of course, if his account of self-esteem were developed within the overall structure of the Gospel, then it would change significantly.

Admittedly, this is a difficult point to communicate and to grasp. As MacIntyre reminds us of his much fuller account of our moral situation, if he is right then "we are in a condition which almost nobody recognises and which perhaps nobody at all can recognise fully."[10] In the same way, if the church has engaged in its own Enlightenment project, then we are in a situation which few recognize and which none recognizes fully.

8. At present a number of theologians are seeking to rehabilitate Schleiermacher's work by overthrowing the traditional reading that I present here. If they succeed, that will not change the force of my argument here, which turns on how Schleiermacher has been read. If Schleiermacher is "revised," then he will become an exemplar of the position I am advocating.

9. Schuller, *Self-Esteem*.

10. MacIntyre, *After Virtue*, 4. That MacIntyre does not himself fully realize our situation is indicated by the fact that he continues to develop and rewrite his arguments in his later works.

One way for us to begin to recognize our situation is by continuing to learn from MacIntyre's account. MacIntyre argues that the Enlightenment project on morality had to fail because it rejected any notion of humanity as we could be if we realized our *telos,* and thus abandoned the very element that gave coherence, meaning, and persuasiveness to our moral precepts. What if the same thing has happened to the Gospel in the church's own Enlightenment project? The church, when it is faithful to the Gospel, gives an account of the present human situation, of humanity as God intends us to be, and of the Gospel of salvation by grace as the means by which humanity moves (or, more properly, is moved) from where we are to where God intends us to be. When the church abandons the teleological conviction of where God intends humanity to be, then we are left with the project of seeking a ground for the claims of the Gospel apart from the Gospel itself. As MacIntyre has shown us, such a project is bound to fail.

Before we move on to consider the consequences of this failure, we should consider an objection, often directed toward MacIntyre, that may be brought against my account. To some, MacIntyre's account, and by extension my account, may appear to give no means for judging among competing convictions and traditions. In other words, our accounts appear fideistic or relativistic. However, as MacIntyre shows in a later work, his position does allow for rational comparison.[11] Moreover, James Wm. McClendon Jr. and James M. Smith have given an extensive account of evaluating and justifying religious convictions that is compatible with the position I am advocating.[12] What our accounts preclude is the notion that there are grounds for justifying the Gospel apart from the Gospel itself.

To go beyond MacIntyre's account, the way for the church to justify the claims of the Gospel is by living the way of life to which the Gospel calls us. This way of life, as it displays the full claims of the Gospel, may then be compared to other ways of life. This comparison occurs, not from some Archimedean point outside every tradition, but from within one's present tradition as one considers the competing claims.[13] In this understanding, the church commends the Gospel by living according to the Gospel, not by appealing to some ground outside the Gospel. For this very

11. MacIntyre, *Three Rival Versions; Whose Justice?*

12. McClendon and Smith, *Convictions.*

13. The best and fullest account of this process may be found in McClendon and Smith, *Convictions.*

reason then, this work is about *living faithfully* in a fragmented world: living faithfully simply *is* the Christian mission in the modern world.

So, one part of the lesson that we learn from MacIntyre's narrative of the failure of the Enlightenment project is that the church has carried on its own version of this project. We will be able to live faithfully in a fragmented world only as we develop our ability to discern how and where we have engaged in this Enlightenment project that is bound to fail.

CONSEQUENCES OF THE FAILURE OF THE ENLIGHTENMENT PROJECT

We may learn something else from MacIntyre's narrative of the failure of the Enlightenment project by attending to one of the consequences of this failure. According to MacIntyre, as a result of this failure, we live in a culture that is marked by three particular "characters." By "characters" MacIntyre means social roles that represent the moral nature of a culture. In these characters, role and personality are fused, and possibilities for action are limited by the culture. These characters provide the members of a culture "with a cultural and moral ideal" that "morally legitimates a mode of social existence."[14] As examples, MacIntyre points to the "Public School Headmaster, Explorer and the Engineer," for Victorian England, and the "Prussian Officer, the Professor and the Social Democrat" for Wilhelmine Germany.[15]

In the emotivist culture that results from the failure of the Enlightenment project, our stock of characters includes the Rich Aesthete, the Therapist, and the Manager.[16] If we consider how these characters mark not only Western culture but also in very particular ways the Western church, we may gain further insight into how the church can live faithfully in a fragmented world.

In MacIntyre's account, the Rich Aesthete, who has a surplus of financial and social resources, seeks to alleviate boredom by manipulating others for the pleasure and good of the Aesthete. MacIntyre rightly warns that not all rich nor all aesthetes live out this character. Nevertheless, our

---

14. MacIntyre, *After Virtue*, 29.

15. Ibid., 28.

16. MacIntyre gives his account of these characters primarily in chapter 3, "Emotivism: Social Content and Social Context," and chapter 6, "Some Consequences of the Failure of the Enlightenment Project."

culture is stocked by this ideal. Even those who do not have the resources to live out this character may aspire to the role: living morally fragmented lives and lacking any clear *telos* for our lives, we may be captured by this character.

In the church, this character of the Rich Aesthete plays itself out in at least two ways. First, in our quest for "converts" we may be motivated more by the manipulation of others to achieve our own ends than by obedience to Christ or the desire to see others find their true *telos* in following Christ. We are especially susceptible to this when our own lives are not oriented toward loving God in obedience. Jesus warns us against this very dynamic in a slightly different setting in Matthew 6: "Beware of practicing your piety before others in order to be seen by them; for then you have no reward from your Father in heaven." In our culture apparently faithful witness may be corrupted by our playing out the role of a religious Rich Aesthete when we seek converts to "add notches" or increase our status before others. Lacking an appropriate *telos*, we manipulate others through the excess of our rhetorical and emotional resources in order to increase our pleasure, alleviate our boredom, and serve our own ends.

We may play out the role of Rich Aesthete in the church in a second way, by seeking our own pleasure in worship. It is certainly right for the church to pursue beauty and excellence in worship, but that pursuit must be oriented first toward glorifying and enjoying God. When we orient worship toward giving ourselves pleasure, either through "high" liturgical worship or through "low" informal worship, we are playing out the role of the Rich Aesthete. Many analyses of what is wrong with our worship fasten on a comparison of high and low worship and argue for the superiority of one over the other. Such analyses usually miss the deeper issue of our cultural context and the subtle temptation to adopt the character of the Rich Aesthete that fulfills a (mistaken) moral ideal and legitimates a larger social mode of existence.

The second character that MacIntyre identifies in our culture is the Therapist.[17] This character has received a great deal of critical attention. In L. Gregory Jones's book, *Embodying Forgiveness*, he devotes a chapter to how the character of the Therapist (with the collusion of the Manager,

17. To be fair, we should note that not all therapists play out the character of the Therapist as MacIntyre describes it. However, given the power of a cultural ideal, we must also recognize how difficult it is to resist this role.

a third character we will consider below), has corrupted our practices of forgiveness.[18] In the previous chapter, I showed how our worship may be wrongly directed toward therapeutic ends. In this chapter, I want to consider briefly the larger problem with the character of the Therapist. As Jones, following MacIntyre, shows, the Therapist plays out our culture's acceptance and reinforcement of "the individualist realm of private feelings and values."[19] That is, as the character of the Therapist is acted out in a morally fragmented culture, the Therapist enables us to adjust our private feelings and values in order to come to terms with that fragmentation. Focusing on technique and lacking any means to question our ends, the Therapist underwrites our moral fragmentation and undermines the possibility of Christian community. Thus, the problem with the Therapist, as acted out in our culture, is not that God wants followers of Jesus to be unhealthy and unhappy; rather, the problem is that the Therapist locates health and happiness in the realm of private feelings and values, not in our discovering and living out the proper *telos* of humanity as revealed in Jesus Christ.

It is important for us to recognize that the role of Therapist may be acted out in formal counseling settings in the church, but it may also be more subtly dangerous in less obvious settings, such as preaching and fellowship. When preaching merely helps us to accept the world in its sin and does not call us to the reality of God's work among us that enables faithful living, then the Therapist has triumphed. When our fellowship is a "conspiracy of cordiality," rather than the communion of the reconciled, the Therapist has triumphed.[20] These triumphs of the Therapist may lead to a growing congregation and apparent success, but they do not lead the Christian community into faithful living.

The third character that MacIntyre identifies in our culture is the Manager. If the Therapist and the Aesthete represent roles in our "private lives" (as demarcated by our culture), the Manager governs our "public lives." According to MacIntyre's analysis, the Manager may be the most pernicious of these characters. For a culture living out the consequences of the failure of the Enlightenment project, the Manager seeks to achieve maximum bureaucratic efficiency without regard to the end. Thus, the

---

18. Jones, *Embodying*, chapter 2.

19. Ibid., 40.

20. Hauerwas and Willimon, *Resident Aliens*, 138.

Manager's authority is justified in our culture, first, by belief in "the existence of a domain of morally neutral fact about which the manager is to be expert." Secondly, the manager is believed to know "law-like generalizations and their applications to particular cases derived from the study of this domain."[21]

The important point about the character of the Manager in our fragmented culture is that the Manager's effectiveness is thought to be morally neutral. That is, the Manager concentrates on mastering "techniques without any evaluation of the ends toward which the techniques are developed."[22] Morality, then, is outside the realm of the Manager's competence and responsibility.

MacIntyre argues that this claim to managerial effectiveness is a "fictitious, but believed-in reality" that is central to our culture. For this reason, he devotes two important chapters to showing the illusory nature of our belief in the domain of morally neutral fact and the predictive power of generalizations in social science to which the Manager claims special access. In this critique, MacIntyre allows modest claims to managerial "effectiveness," but disputes the larger claims to managerial power that so often mark our culture. The persistence of those larger claims and our acceptance of them, he shows, depend upon the moral fragmentation of our culture and the "histrionic skills" of the Manager (whom MacIntyre sometimes labels "the bureaucrat"): "The most effective manager is the best actor."[23] By this claim, MacIntyre means that despite the illusory basis of the Manager's claim to authority, that authority may be maintained by the Manager's ability to sustain the illusion by acting it out convincingly.

As the Western church participates in the consequences of the failure of the Enlightenment project, it may be infected by the character of the Manager. This infection may be difficult to diagnose, because we do not think of the church as a domain of morally neutral fact ruled by law-like generalizations from the social sciences. However, in our morally fragmented world, the church may often find itself serving ends other than faithfulness to God. In this situation, the church may appear successful and the Manager may appear effective, but that success and effectiveness can be directed toward wrong ends.

21. MacIntyre, *After Virtue*, 77.

22. Jones, *Embodying*, 40.

23. MacIntyre, *After Virtue*, 108.

Before continuing, we should note two qualifications. First, it is not success or effectiveness that is problematic. Rather the problem is that in our culture "success" and "effectiveness" are determined by the illusory convictions outlined above. Certainly, the church is called to be successful and effective, but it is called to be those things in relation to the mission given by God, not by our culture. Second, as I move on to criticize the church's use of the social sciences, that criticism is directed toward the practice of social science that is divorced from the question of ends and strives merely for maximum bureaucratic effectiveness.[24]

The church's capitulation to the authority of the Manager is tied to the centrality of that character in our culture and to the church's attempt to live with its history. Seeking to recover or to maintain our perceived place in the culture, we in the church turn to the Manager for guidance. So today, some of the most powerful leaders of the church are those who know how to manage public opinion and the political process in order to achieve success. If we examine the ends of that management, however, we may well question whether its "success" is directed toward making disciples.

Although the influence of the Church Growth Movement and its advocacy of the "homogeneous unit principle" is fading, at one time this movement represented a powerful example of the authority of the Manager. Drawing largely on social science, this movement argued that the most effective means for growing churches was through targeting "homogeneous units." The social scientific apparatus that accompanied this argument and its apparent effectiveness drew many churches into its orbit. Today, most advocates of this movement have greatly modified their position and propose modest claims more in line with MacIntyre's analysis of managerial effectiveness. Nevertheless, the movement stands as a reminder of the church's capitulation to the character of the Manager.

Finally, drawing on MacIntyre's analysis of the character of the Manager, we can learn to be on guard against the perpetuation of the authority of the Manager through histrionics. In recent years, many sincere followers of Jesus Christ have been made captive to "good acting." What else are the televangelists but prime examples of MacIntyre's dictum that "the most effective bureaucrat is the best actor?" Quite apart from these

24. In a *tour de force*, John Milbank deconstructs theological reliance on social theory and relocates social questions within ecclesiology in Milbank, *Theology*.

highly visible Managers, many local churches aspire to have pastors who differ from televangelists only in the degree of acting ability they possess and in the private morality they live out. That is, they do not see the pernicious effect of the Manager on the church's faithfulness. They want a pastor who combines managerial effectiveness with private morality.

THE THIRD LESSON

The Western church has lived through the failure of the Enlightenment project in the culture and in its own life. We now live with the consequences of that failure. As MacIntyre warns us, that failure and its consequences are difficult to discern. Many good and wonderful things are entangled with much unfaithfulness and destructiveness. To exercise discernment and to recover faithful living will require effort by each of us—the exercise of the gifts of the Spirit in the body of Christ.

At this point, we have learned that living with our history means that we live with fragments of morality and Christian discipleship that result from the failure of the Enlightenment project of morality. In this place and time, the full import of our situation is nearly impossible for us to discern clearly and fully. We can easily mistake a collection of fragments for something fuller, but what we actually have is only the appearance of faithful living—a simulacrum—not its reality.

In this situation, new monastic communities are one of the most important settings for us to learn how to overcome the failure of the Enlightenment project of morality and its effect on the church. In new monastic communities, we can more faithfully identify, resist, and overcome the consequences of the Enlightenment project as these communities follow a rule and live in close enough proximity to one another to discern their susceptibility to the consequences of the Enlightenment project identified above. This is a not to claim that new monastic communities will somehow be purer or less susceptible, but that the form of their life and its teleology will allow them to identify and by the Spirit overcome the Enlightenment project and its consequences. As they seek this faithfulness to the gospel, they will face a major temptation that must be carefully identified even as they learn from MacIntyre's work some of the ways of faithfulness. So we turn in the next chapter to the Nietzschean temptation before we explore the path of faithful living in a fragmented world.

FOUR

Resisting the Nietzschean Temptation

The pivotal chapter in *After Virtue* is chapter 9, "Nietzsche or Aristotle?"
Here MacIntyre lays out the absolute choice that we face: will we follow
Nietzsche or Aristotle? Nietzsche is the inevitable outcome of the failure
of the Enlightenment project. If we cannot construct a viable morality on
the basis that the Enlightenment sought to lay down, then we are left with
only "the will to power." If we refuse to follow this path, then according to
After Virtue the only other path available to us is Aristotle.

In the next two chapters we will explore the Aristotelian path with
MacIntyre, though we will be drawing on his insights to blaze another
trail, one that follows Jesus Christ rather than Aristotle. In this chapter,
we will explore the Nietzschean path to discern its temptations and the
ways that we may indeed stray onto this path as a result of our own history with modernity.[1]

The Nietzschean temptation takes two forms. The first is the temptation to reduce everything to morality. This temptation is not original
with Nietzsche; we may trace it back at least to Immanuel Kant's turn to
practical reason, but it has its practitioners scattered throughout history.
What MacIntyre's account has shown us is the outcome of such reduction
in the Enlightenment project. The second temptation is the reduction of
everything to power. Again, this temptation is not original to Nietzsche

---

1. This chapter is an addition to this revised edition of *Living Faithfully*. At the time
that I wrote the first edition I did not see so clearly the lure of Nietzsche. I analyze and
resist much of the Nietzschean temptation under the description "postmodernity" in
Gospel Virtues, but our present situation calls for continuing analysis and resistance.

(cf. Luke 4:5–8), but it does become a highly developed theme in his work, which at the same time is directed with energetic disdain toward the weakness of Christianity. These two temptations may be roughly described as modernist and postmodernist, though they are not the only temptations present in these two eras and cultural moods. That they both come to us in Nietzsche signifies his importance as a pivotal character in the turn from modernity to postmodernity.

THE FIRST TEMPTATION

The first temptation that the Nietzschean alternative presents is the temptation to reduce everything to morality. MacIntyre does not so clearly and directly identify this mistake in *After Virtue* as he does in later works.[2] But the temptation is clearly present. Indeed, if one succumbs to the reduction of everything to mere morality, then the second Nietzschean temptation follows inexorably. That is, if there is no reason(s) for one's morality, then morality is simply an expression of the will.[3] But before we follow that development, we must consider this first temptation.

The temptation to reduce everything to mere morality is powerful for at least two reasons. First, it is one possible result of the rediscovery that practices are at the heart of following Jesus Christ. Many today have rightly discovered that beliefs are not enough, that assent to a set of propositions is not sufficient for Christian faith. Positively, many of us have become convinced that doctrine is also ethics—again also rightly. For those who have come to these convictions, it is an easy but wrong step to conclude that everything is ethics or morality.

In the face of this temptation, it is vital to recognize the structure of MacIntyre's argument and the insight that it gives us into Christian discipleship. We will explore MacIntyre's constructive proposal more fully in the next chapter, but here we may note that for MacIntyre the recovery of morality depends upon a whole structure of rationality grounded in a particular tradition. One factor in the failure of the Enlightenment proj-

2. In fact, one could argue that *Whose Justice? Which Rationality?* is written in part to fill in this gap, with its concentration on developing an alternative account of the rationality of traditions. Of course, this later work also moves beyond Aristotle to Aquinas.

3. For this reason I worry about works such as Lewis Smedes's *Mere Morality*, which for all its wisdom, seems to disconnect "mere morality" from the prior action of God in Israel's history. The reason for living according to the Ten Commandments is to enjoy life with the God who has begun the work of salvation.

ect of morality was its attempt to separate morality from any particular tradition. But beyond this failure, we must also see the failure entailed in reducing everything to morality.

For MacIntyre, any morality that seeks to claim reasons for its practice does so on the basis of a tradition that embodies a conviction about the *telos* for human beings that calls for certain practices that form particular virtues in its practitioners. Thus, morality is part of a whole vision of life, but that vision cannot be reduced to morality.

For the church, our morality—our way of life—is an inextricable part of our faith. Morality is not an optional addition to a set of propositions that are the only necessity to our faith. It is not that we have "beliefs" or "doctrines" that are necessary to our faith and "actions" or "ethics" that are optional. If we understand our beliefs and doctrines properly, then they also entail actions and ethics. But this insight, which is an important rediscovery today, must not lead us to reduce our faith to morality. To say that morality is a necessary element of our faith is not the same as saying that morality is the end of our faith.

For Christians today there is a great temptation to reduce our faith to morality. As we learn to live with our history, bring coherence to our fragmented lives, and recover from emotivism (the outcome of the Enlightenment project of morality), we are drawn to the crucial importance of morality in our faithful witness to the good news of Jesus Christ. This is right and necessary; but in living out this discovery we must not lose sight of the conviction that we are seeking to recover our life as disciples of Jesus Christ precisely in order to witness to him as the way, the truth, and the life. It is this purpose that gives our morality its meaning beyond the sheer exercise of will.

The second reason that we are tempted to reduce everything to morality is that it seems to promise us the possibility of overcoming so many things that divide us. Surely on the basis of shared moral convictions we can find common ground with those who do not share our convictions about Jesus Christ. Surely, here in ethics, we can set aside other differences and agree on questions of justice.

This temptation is strong for those of us who have been formed by separatist Christian communities. When we discover that Christian faith should be lived in public and not in an isolated, protected, gated spiritual community, we may think that the only way for us to live in public is by finding common moral ground rather than risking the actual living out of our convictions about Jesus Christ in public. Surely we can see that what Jesus really calls us to is a morality that does not depend upon his particular identity for its meaning.

In new monastic communities, these temptations may be particularly strong. For one thing, new monastic communities are formed by convictions about the Christian faith and the necessity of recovering particular ways of living that take on the appearance of morality. In light of this, these communities may be quite susceptible to forgetting that their reason for existence is the recovery of faithful lives of discipleship to Jesus Christ. When they forget this practice of discipleship, these communities have already essentially reduced their lives to morality even though that reduction and its effects may not be immediately evident.

The history of the church, especially in the twentieth century, is littered with the wreckage of Christian communities that forgot the vision and convictions that formed and gave them life.[4] When they reduce their life to morality without the tradition, *telos*, practices, and virtues that generate and sustain a way of life, then their morality devolves, as MacIntyre shows us, into emotivism and a bare will to power. Such developments are signs of the inexorable dissolution of community and witness to the gospel apart from God's judging and restoring grace.

New monastic communities need to be especially aware of one particular dynamic of this reductionist temptation. The dynamic that concerns me is the possible impulse in new monastic communities to respond to accusations of sectarianism by reducing the vision and life of new monastic communities to a morality that allows them to participate in the public sphere without regard for the reality of the gospel that calls them into existence.

There are a number of subtle dimensions to this temptation. First, we must note that new monastic communities do not exist in isolation from society as a means of establishing a pure community life. Rather, new monastic communities exist in the midst of society and live their life in the midst of society as a witness to the gospel. The monastic impulse at its best was never a withdrawal from society for the sake of their own purity, but rather an intentional concentration of relationships and discipline for the sake of faithful witness to the gospel for the sake of the world's salvation.

---

4. In many instances, communities were formed with very little, if any, of the kind of reflection and conviction that we are engaged with here.

So new monastic communities have a deep commitment to avoiding "sectarianism" understood as a withdrawal from society and an isolated quest for purity. This means that they are sensitive to accusations of sectarianism. Such sensitivity may lead them to over-react to such accusations by reducing their convictions to a moral program that supposedly does not require Christian faith for its meaning.

At the same time, new monastic communities are committed to public faithfulness to the gospel. That is, they are committed to participation in society always on the basis of their prior participation in and commitment to Jesus Christ. One of the fragmentations that new monastic communities seek healing for is the belief that life in Jesus Christ characterizes a private, personal realm and that life in the public realm is ruled by something separate from our life in Christ, such as a general, shared concept of justice. New monastic communities seek to live in faithfulness to Christ in all realms of life. Thus, for example, the forgiveness and mercy of Christ governs our practices in all of life, as does his justice. It is not justice for the public realm and mercy in private, it is justice and mercy in all of life.

For new monastic communities, this means that they must resist the temptation to play down the convictions that guide their practices. Indeed, the very practices that they engage in, even in "public," are means for them to participate more fully in God's work in the world and to bear witness to it. If they succumb to the reductionist temptation, they will have abandoned the holistic vision that calls them into existence and sustains them in integral mission.

One final complication marks this dynamic. New monastic communities are committed to living in public as witnesses to the gospel in all of life as an alternative to other social structures. This means that they do not look to the state or to other social structures as the primary means of fulfilling God's purposes in the world. Certainly, these other structures are ordained by God and under God's rule in justice and mercy. But it is in and through God's people that God's rule is made known. As we have noted in chapter 2, this is true when God's people are faithful *and* when we are unfaithful. In both cases, God makes God's will known to the world through the people whom God has chosen as witnesses.

For new monastic communities, this means that they do not regard themselves as advisors to other agents who then carry out God's will.

The Second Temptation

The second Nietzschean temptation is both more obvious and more natural than the first. As the first temptation represents the modern element in the Nietzschean turn, so the second temptation represents the postmodern element in the Nietzschean turn. In this postmodern turn, the second temptation seeks to lure the church and new monastic communities into a struggle for power as the fundamental characteristic of life and the mark of responsible participation in the world.

This temptation draws some of its power from the failure of the Enlightenment project. Since the Enlightenment project on morality has failed, we are left with an emotivist morality. That is, moral statements are merely statements of feeling or emotion disguised as statements of fact or statements of value derived from fact. Once we strip away the disguise, we can see clearly that all we have left is the attempt to gain power, protect power, or conceal power.

This is the "will to power" identified by Nietzsche with such devastating clarity and force. This Nietzschean will to power is not the will of the individual, but rather is that of a larger, impersonal reality that marks and ultimately controls all of life. Nietzscheans argue that this will to power is disguised by the fiction of an individual will. For Nietzscheans, this fiction conceals the true will to power. It misleads us into thinking that we can actually will good and evil. But if the Enlightenment project has failed, then there is no good and evil, there are simply emotions that we use to fabricate the labels "good" and "evil." And often that fabrication is the work of self-delusion that needs to be exposed so that the inescapable will to power is acknowledged.

In this situation, the disciple community faces a number of temptations. One temptation that the church faces is to capitulate to this second Nietzschean temptation and accept that everything is just about power—gained, protected, or concealed. In this capitulation, new monastic communities may come to be regarded as the church's new and brilliant strategy for surviving, succeeding, and even thriving in this new circumstance. In other words, new monastic communities would be seen as the product of social analysis, strategy, and planning that seeks to gain power for the church and its agenda.

We could be led into this temptation by a possible reading of MacIntyre's description of the circumstances that lead to our waiting "for another—doubtless very different—St. Benedict."[5] In the passage preceding these concluding words, MacIntyre seems to present this cryptic call for a new monasticism as a survival strategy for the new dark ages. We do not need to determine the best interpretation of MacIntyre's call in order to identify this temptation and its mistake.

If MacIntyre is slipping into a commendation of new monasticism as a survival strategy, he has made two errors. First, he is contradicting his own argument about "Fact, Explanation, and Expertise" and "The Character of Generalizations in Social Science and Their Lack of Predictive Power."[6] In these chapters he argues that "systematic unpredictability in human affairs" makes unsupportable the claims to managerial and bureaucratic expertise that mark our quests for power and control.[7] These claims to expertise, grounded in the social sciences, fail because of "the nature of radical conceptual innovation, unforeseen consequences of unmade decisions, the game-theoretic character of life, and pure contingency."[8] These arguments by MacIntyre mean that we are mistaken if we ground a call to new monastic communities in managerial insight or pragmatic calculation.

Secondly, if MacIntyre is commending new monastic communities as a survival strategy, he is also misrepresenting the nature of monasticism and new monasticism. These movements did not arise out of a desire to survive and succeed but out of a desire to be faithful. The focus for these communities is on God not the world, on faithfulness not success, and on the weakness and foolishness of following the crucified Messiah not gaining power in the world. Here we must recognize the call to faithfulness that does not calculate the chances of success or analyze the cost-benefit ratio, but rather asks how we may most faithfully participate in the *telos* into which we are called.

These reflections on the Nietzschean temptation faced by new monastic communities should also reveal to us how much the church, especially in Western cultures, has already succumbed to this temptation. We can see this in the ways that the church simply adopts social sciences as means to accomplish the church's programs and acquire power for the

---

5. MacIntyre, *After Virtue*, 263.

6. MacIntyre, *After Virtue*, chapters 7 and 8.

7. Ibid., 93.

8. Ibid., 93–100.

church in the context of postmodern culture. This is a subtle temptation for two reasons. First, there is a modest role for social sciences to
play in human affairs. However, given the failure of the Enlightenment
project of morality and the consequent turn to power, modesty is a virtue
seldom cultivated today. And where it is initially cultivated, it is soon
wiped out by the demands of power in social settings. This is true even
of churches and seminaries, where modesty and unpretentiousness are
rarely exemplified.

The other (perhaps not-so) subtle temptation of the social sciences's
promise of power and control is rooted in our history. As we saw in
chapter 2, the church has moved from a place of perceived influence in
Western society to a place on the margins of our society. There is a great
temptation in the power and control promised by the social sciences to
provide the resources for the church to regain its place of influence in
our society.

This temptation plays itself out not only in the church as a whole
but can also become a mark of new monastic communities. One of the
challenges to new monastic communities is to have or develop the discipline to be faithful in small and uncelebrated ways. As an unfamiliar and
sometimes "exotic" manifestation of Christianity, new monastic communities may receive attention from the media—as they have in cover
stories from *Christian Century, Christianity Today*, and other magazines
as well as newspapers. This attention is a mixed blessing and needs to be
recognized as a possible source of temptation. If getting in the news or
staying in the news becomes a measure of success or faithfulness for new
monastic communities, then their very calling has been abandoned.

In the midst of media attention and coming to terms with our
history, it is also tempting for new monastic communities to present
themselves or to allow themselves to be presented as "getting it right" or
"doing it better" or "correcting past mistakes." None of these are appropriate descriptions of new monasticism. Rather, these communities come
together simply because of the way they are seeking to live is the gospel.
Their vision is not a rejection of the past (as we often saw in the Christian
communes and renewal movements of the 60s), but an embrace of the
past and an acceptance of responsibility for our history.

FIVE

Recovering Tradition[1]

In the first chapter we considered what the church might learn from MacIntyre for living faithfully in a fragmented world by learning to live with our history. In chapters 2 and 3 we considered what the church might learn from MacIntyre's narrative of the failure of the Enlightenment project and the consequences of that failure. In chapter 4, we examined two forms of the Nietzschean temptation that new monastic communities may face in order to expose them and disarm them. In this and the concluding chapter we will consider what the church might learn from a second story narrated by MacIntyre.

THE "ARISTOTELIAN" STORY

In *After Virtue*, MacIntyre develops his argument by telling two stories.[2] The first story, "the failure of the Enlightenment project," has already given us a number of lessons. The second story MacIntyre tells is of the classical tradition of morality. In telling this story MacIntyre seeks to vindicate and recover a form of the Aristotelian moral tradition. MacIntyre's narrative of this tradition begins with the earliest Greek poets of heroic

---

1. Here we turn to MacIntyre's constructive counter-proposal to the Enlightenment project. This proposal could be characterized in a number of ways, each of which has its limitations. I have chosen "tradition" as a way of faithfully reflecting the development of MacIntyre's proposal beyond *After Virtue*. See MacIntyre, *Whose Justice* and *Three Rival Versions*.

2. This and the following three paragraphs are adapted from Wilson, *Living Faithfully* (1990), 40–41.

society and then moves on to the dramatists and philosophers of early Athenian society. After MacIntyre scrutinizes Aristotle's detailed account of this moral tradition, he considers the medieval "dialogue with"—rather than "simple assent to"—the Aristotelian moral tradition.[3] MacIntyre argues that this dialogue brought three improvements to the classical moral tradition: (1) it recognized the inevitability of conflict and met conflict with the Christian virtues of charity and forgiveness, which were entirely missing in Aristotle; (2) its understanding of God's grace meant that neither Aristotle's *fortuna* (the bad luck of ugliness, low birth, childlessness, or other such circumstances) nor evil (provided we do not become complicit) excludes anyone from realizing the human good; (3) it incorporated a fuller understanding of human historicity—Aristotle understood that the moral life is lived in a particular place; the medieval thinkers recognized that the moral life is also lived within a particular history.

This is the moral tradition the Enlightenment sought to escape. Now that we see the failure of the Enlightenment project, MacIntyre advocates a recovery of some form of the Aristotelian tradition. His constructive proposal consists of five elements: the conception of a practice, an account of the virtues, a narrative account of the good life (the *telos*) for a human, a living tradition, and a community within which these are set. MacIntyre spends several chapters developing and defending his proposal. He contrasts his position to competitors, defends it against objections, and argues for its viability, even its necessity.

A REVISION OF MACINTYRE

MacIntyre's proposal provides us with several lessons for living faithfully in a fragmented world. However, before we turn to those lessons, we must consider a weakness in MacIntyre's proposal as it stands in *After Virtue*. MacIntyre has since revised and expanded his argument, most notably in *Whose Justice? Which Rationality?* Nevertheless, to make full use of his proposal for the church, we must revise it.[4]

The weakness in MacIntyre's account in *After Virtue* is that, although he advocates a recovery of the moral tradition, no specific moral tradi-

3. MacIntyre, *After Virtue*, 165.

4. Even with this later work, MacIntyre has still received considerable criticism or his neglect of substantive theological convictions (Jones, *Transformed Judgment*; Milbank, *Theology and Social Theory*; Hauerwas and Pinches, *Christians*). The major purpose of my revision of MacIntyre's proposal will be to give some theological direction.

tion is present.[5] He argues for a conception of practices but advocates no specific practices. He argues for virtues but no particular virtues. His proposal, as it stands in *After Virtue*, is a torso without a head, onto which any number of heads may be grafted. John Rawls, for example, has given an account of liberal democracy, the development of which is inextricably tied to the Enlightenment project that MacIntyre decries, as a tradition with practices and virtues set within a community.[6]

Thus, MacIntyre's account in *After Virtue* must be revised. In part, I think this weakness is due to the fact that *After Virtue* represents a stage in MacIntyre's return to Christianity. As I have already noted, MacIntyre himself revises his account in later writing. Nevertheless, his account gives us some guidance for living faithfully in a fragmented world, to which we will add some theological substance.[7] Although the five elements of MacIntyre's proposal fit tightly together, for the sake of clarity we will consider them separately and then weave them back together.

Before turning to our constructive account, I must add one more caveat. If MacIntyre's account of our circumstances is generally accurate, as I believe it is, then this constructive account will lack initial plausibility because we are in a situation in which it has few exemplars. That is, the real force of MacIntyre's constructive proposal rests in its embodiment in the life of a community. Lacking communities that exhibit such force, accounts such as mine can only grope toward living faithfully. In the end, it is not my account but faithful communities that will teach us how to live faithfully in a fragmented world. Nevertheless, drawing on MacIntyre's insights, we may gain some understanding of what we are groping toward, by God's grace.

THE GOOD LIFE

In MacIntyre's account, he shows that our moral fragmentation largely results from the loss of the conception of the *telos* of human life. Since this loss is at the heart of our fragmentation, it is helpful to begin our

5. Some of the material in this paragraph is adapted from Wilson, *Living Faithfully* (1990).

6. Rawls, *Political Liberalism*, Part III, Lecture IV. MacIntyre himself later acknowledges the "tradition" of liberalism and subjects it to critique in MacIntyre, *Whose Justice*, chapter 17.

7. See my further development of theological substance in Wilson, *Gospel Virtues* and *Why Church Matters*.

constructive account at this point. In *After Virtue*, MacIntyre provisionally defines the *telos*, or "good life," for humans, as "the life spent in seeking for the good life for man."[8] Although this conclusion is provisional, MacIntyre gives little further explanation in *After Virtue*. In spite of the rather abstract account MacIntyre gives of the good life, he does make clear that we must recover some notion of the *telos* of humanity.

The Christian notion of the human *telos* may be described in various ways. In MacIntyre's later work, he moves toward a more Christian and theological conception of the good life by drawing on Thomas Aquinas's assertion that the human *telos* is "that state of perfect happiness which is the contemplation of God in the beatific vision."[9] In an earlier discussion, I drew on the Westminster Catechism's teaching that the true end of humanity is "to glorify God and enjoy him forever." We may add to this Paul's assertion that the purpose of God's work is that "all of us come to the unity of the faith and of the knowledge of the Son of God, to maturity, to the measure of the full stature of Christ" (Ephesians 4:13, NRSV). Although these statements use different language and images, they give compatible descriptions of the human *telos* revealed in the Gospel of Jesus Christ.[10]

The lesson for the church to learn from MacIntyre is that we must revitalize our ability to give an account of the good life for humans that is revealed in the Gospel. This revitalization will not end conflict; indeed, it may heighten conflict. But at the same time, on MacIntyre's account, it will enable us to locate those conflicts properly. In so doing, it will also enable us to live more faithfully by the Gospel rather than the Enlightenment project.

The most important lesson to learn from MacIntyre about our attempts to give a Christian account of the good life is that we must learn to live and to think "teleologically." That is, Christians must seek continually to give an account of our lives that coheres with our *telos*. In so doing we can resist, and even overcome, the moral fragmentation of our lives by continually seeking to order our lives toward our conception of the human *telos*. In other words, we must learn to give an account not just of

8. MacIntyre, *After Virtue*, 220.

9. MacIntyre, *Whose Justice*, 192.

10. In the section below on "living tradition," I will consider further the arguments within the church over different accounts of the human *telos*.

what Christians do, but also of why we do it in relation to the conception of the human *telos* revealed in the Gospel.

This kind of living and thinking examines our practices to see if they are coherent with our understanding of God's purposes for humanity. Take, for example, the Church Growth Movement. Can we give an account of how practicing the "homogeneous unit principle" coheres with Paul's call to unity in Christ, which occurs in the same letter in which he describes the crumbling of the wall between Jew and Gentile (Ephesians 2)? Or consider our practices of forgiveness. Are they ordered toward therapeutic happiness, managerial control, or reconciliation in Christ? At all points in our lives, we must ask whether our lives are directed toward maturity in Christ or toward some other competing, and often unrecognized, *telos*.

MacIntyre, then, teaches us to think teleologically, to identify the human *telos* and order our lives toward it. Such ordering cannot be sustained alone; it requires the other elements of MacIntyre's proposal. Since, as noted above, the quest to identify the human *telos* may intensify rather than reduce conflict, we turn now to MacIntyre's account of this kind of conflict.

THE LIVING TRADITION

According to MacIntyre, a living tradition "is an historically extended, socially embodied argument, and an argument precisely in part about the goods which constitute that tradition."[11] In this description, MacIntyre acknowledges that teleological thinking brings conflict—precisely over the *telos* toward which our thinking should be ordered. But he also places that conflict within the large context of a "living tradition," which is constituted by both the nature of the conflict and what counts as important within it.

If we recover this understanding of living tradition for living faithfully in a fragmented world, we will begin to discern ways in which the church has been corrupted in Western culture. We will begin to recover arguments, like the ones noted above, over whether this or that practice of the church is oriented toward the proper end. We will also begin to argue about what constitutes that proper end.

11. MacIntyre, *After Virtue*, 222.

In these arguments, we must learn from MacIntyre how to understand the "rationality" of tradition. First, we must learn what it means to participate in a *living* tradition. In MacIntyre's account, a living tradition may be conservative, but it is not static. Over time tensions and contradictions may arise internally and externally. A living tradition responds to these tensions and contradictions in various ways. Some traditions decay over time and lose their potency—they die. Others emerge from such challenges stronger than ever.

In Acts 15, we have a wonderful example of the church's participation in a living tradition. There the early church confronts an apparent contradiction: faith in Christ and the presence of the Holy Spirit have been given to uncircumcised Gentiles. These events are a profound challenge to the tradition of the church. Yet, as John Howard Yoder shows, they respond to this challenge from within the tradition and emerge faithful and strong.[12] The conflict does not end, but it now takes place as a "socially embodied argument" about the goods—in particular, one good, circumcision—that constitute the tradition.

The second lesson we must learn from MacIntyre's account of a living tradition is to recognize the difference between the rationality of a tradition over against other forms of rationality. In the work that follows *After Virtue*, MacIntyre devotes much energy to this topic.[13] This topic is too complex to give a full account here. Suffice it to say that in the Gospel the church not only has a living tradition but an ever-present reality. That is, the Gospel is not merely something from the past that continues to live on in the memory of the church; it is also, and more significantly, the redeeming work of God in Jesus Christ present in the past and present today. The church's calling is to discern that present reality and live faithfully in it. Thus, the life of the church embodies the rationality of the Gospel.

In a church marked by the moral fragmentation of the Enlightenment project, such an outcome cannot occur. But in a church that is seeking to be faithful to a living tradition under the guidance of the Holy Spirit, such an outcome is promised. However, the existence of such a church depends upon further elements in MacIntyre's proposal.

---

12. Yoder, *Priestly Kingdom*, 15–45.
13. MacIntyre, *Whose Justice*, chapter 18, and *Three Rival Versions*.

PRACTICES

In MacIntyre's proposal, "practice" takes on a very specific meaning. In a lengthy and complex description, MacIntyre defines a practice as

> any coherent and complex form of socially established cooperative human activity through which goods internal to that form of activity are realized in the course of trying to achieve those standards of excellence which are appropriate to, and partially definitive of, that form of activity, with the result that human powers to achieve excellence, and human conception of the goods involved, are systematically extended.[14]

From the many things that we may learn from this definition for living faithfully, I will draw out three.[15]

First, we must simply learn to think of the church's activities as practices in MacIntyre's sense. Many, if not most, of the church's activities today lack this understanding of practice. We do many things as a church, but we would find it difficult to give an account of how those activities reflect our conception of the human good and how those activities constitute the church as a community.

For example, as I noted in an earlier chapter, the form and style of worship is a source of conflict in many churches today. It is often difficult to see this conflict as anything other than an expression of personal preference. If we formulated the conflict in terms of MacIntyre's practice, then we would better be able to locate the conflict appropriately in relation the goods of the church and the enhancement of our ability to conceive and extend those goods. In this understanding of our conflicts over worship, "excellence" in worship would be defined in ways "appropriate to, and partially definitive of," the practice of worship—not of, say, group therapy, entertainment, or a motivational rally.

Second, we must learn from MacIntyre's notion of practice the importance of "internal goods." As noted in chapter 2, in a morally fragmented culture we often orient our activities toward goods or ends that are external to that activity. In MacIntyre's account of practice, he exposes that mistake. Of course, a practice may lead to goods external to

---

14. MacIntyre, *After Virtue*, 187.

15. For further reflection on Christian practices that draw on MacIntyre, see Tilley, "In Favor"; Jones, *Transformed Judgment*; Hauerwas, *After Christendom*; McClendon, *Ethics, Convictions*; and Murphy et al., *Virtues*.

the practice, but the integrity of the practice as practice depends upon the achievement of goods internal to the practice.

To return to our previous example, someone may play basketball to achieve goods internal to basketball, such as physical exercise or camaraderie. Or one may play basketball for goods external to basketball, such as winning a college scholarship or achieving fame and fortune. In the first instance, basketball is a practice; in the second instance, it is not. Likewise, in the church we may engage in activities as practices or we may transform our activities into something else. We may, for example, engage in evangelistic activities as a practice to achieve goods internal to that practice: attaining the unity of faith, full knowledge of Christ, and maturity as believers. Or we may transform those activities into something else by seeking to increase our "giving base," having the largest church in town, or increasing our reputation and influence in the denomination. If we learn from MacIntyre to think of the activities of the church as practices, then we will be better equipped to live faithfully in a fragmented world.

Third, we must learn from MacIntyre's conception of practice the need to extend our conception of the good and our powers to achieve that good. In other words, practice takes time and discipline. One of the mistakes of the Enlightenment is to think that moral action and moral community are simply the product of a decision to act morally. That is, in spite of my previous history of acting immorally, I can, in the moment, decide to act morally and actually do so. To be sure, the Gospel teaches us that we who are sinners can, by God's grace, be made righteous. But there is also great emphasis on transformation, on growing toward maturity. In theological terms, we are sanctified by the work of the Holy Spirit.

MacIntyre's description of practice gives us an understanding of this process of growth in sanctification that illumines our circumstances so that we may live faithfully with our history as church in Western culture. Faithful living is not achieved in a moment or through mastering technique. Rather, faithful living is a life-long process of "practicing church" as we embody and extend the human *telos* revealed in the Gospel as well as our powers to participate in that *telos*.[16]

16. I recognize that my account of practice here is somewhat cryptic and abstract. That is necessarily so within the confines of this book. My account is extended in Wilson, *Why Church Matters*. However, no matter how extensive an account one might give of Christian practice, such practice must ultimately take place in actual communities of believers.

VIRTUES

The virtues, according to MacIntyre, are

> to be understood as those dispositions which will not only sustain practices and enable us to achieve the goods internal to practices, but will also sustain us in the relevant kind of quest for the good, by enabling us to overcome the harms, dangers, temptations, and distractions which we will encounter, and which will furnish us with increasing self-knowledge and knowledge of the good.[17]

MacIntyre's retrieval of "virtue ethics" has received considerable scrutiny from Christian theologians and ethicists. Since the language of virtue is almost entirely missing from the New Testament and since virtue often, though not necessarily, tends to place undue emphasis on human ability to achieve the good apart from God's grace, the language of virtue needs to be transfigured for the church's use.[18]

Perhaps the most helpful way for the church to use MacIntyre's proposal is to use the language of character, habituation, and disposition. This language emphasizes that our practices are best thought of, not as momentary exercises of the will, but as activities that *pattern* our life in discipleship to Jesus Christ.[19] This patterning of our lives on the life of Jesus Christ creates in believers the character and the habits that are ordered toward our true *telos*.[20]

This language helps us attend to our history as we seek to live faithfully. In contrast to an account of Christian living that focuses on momentary obedience, patterning our lives in Christ teaches us to live teleologically, with a view to where we are headed. As Paul argues in Colossians 3, if our destiny is hidden in Christ, then our lives here and now should be ordered toward that future. At the same time, this emphasis on character also teaches us to attend to our past. When we come to Christ, we come as people formed by many different goods. Those habits we have acquired over the years undergo transformation through our discipleship to Christ.

17. MacIntyre, *After Virtue*, 2–19.

18. See Hauerwas, *Character*; Hauerwas and Pinches, *Christians*; McClendon, *Ethics*; Jones, *Transformed Judgment*.

19. Jones, *Transformed Judgment*, 110–12.

20. As with my account of practice, I am aware here that my account of virtue or character remains somewhat cryptic and abstract. I develop this in *Gospel Virtues*, where I will give an extensive account of the central Christian virtues of faith, hope, and love, and the practices that sustain those virtues.

We acquire new habits as we engage in the practices of the church. If we do not recognize the force of our prior history and habits, we can easily become discouraged by our initial attempts at discipleship. In a culture that prizes the "mastery of technique," we must learn from MacIntyre to prize Christian discipleship as the life-long practice and acquisition of the character that transforms our lives in Christ-likeness.

COMMUNITY

In many ways this entire book is an argument, drawn from MacIntyre, about the nature of the church as a community in the context of a morally fragmented society. Therefore, for the church to be a community we must learn to live with our history, in a morally fragmented culture, amid the failure of the Enlightenment project. In order to do this, we must reclaim our understanding of the human *telos* revealed in the Gospel, participate in the living tradition of Christian faith, and embody that *telos* and that tradition in our practices and virtues (character). From these assertions, we may draw out three characteristics of the church as community.

First, the church must be a community that stands over against the world for the sake of the world. Since the church lives by a *telos* different from the various *telē* of the world, if the church is living faithfully it simply will stand over against the world. However, since the church's *telos* is to witness to God's love for the world in Jesus Christ, the church's life is also for the sake of the world. In the many debates about the relationship between the church and the world, the import of this teleology is often missing. If the church is to be faithful to the Gospel, it cannot do other than stand over against the world. Of course, even the faithful church will often look like the world. Our dress, our language, our architecture, our organization, and other elements will be drawn from our culture. But if we have a strong conception of the human good that is rooted in the Gospel, then our use of these cultural elements will be significantly transformed. Moreover, to live faithfully the church must be explicit about its transformation of these elements for its own life and for its witness to the Gospel.

Second, the church as a community must stand over against the world for the sake of the world. Since the church's conception of the human *telos* is a *telos* for all humanity, the church's faithfulness in living out that *telos* is the means by which the world may discover its true end and enter into the grace of God. In this way, then, the life of the church is given up for the salvation of the world just as Jesus Christ gave up his life for our salvation. In this way, the church "preaches the Gospel" through a life lived over against the world.

Third, the church as a community lives by the grace of God. It is called into existence by the work of God in the Holy Spirit. Once we were "not a people," but now we are "God's people" (1 Peter 2:10). As God's people, we are called to point beyond ourselves. Our *telos* is not the survival and success of the church; rather, our *telos* lies beyond even the church:

> But the church cannot and will not preach this word unless it is ready, with true, yea, and fiery, evangelical zeal, to point beyond itself to the kingdom of God. . . . [W]e can say, and we must say, that to join a church may provoke a hunger for a higher righteousness. It may create an awareness of the demand for a world-transcending loyalty, and it may open the eyes for the first time upon the possibilities of communion with God in Christ. We go about seeking those who for these ultimate reasons will identify themselves with those who love Christ and love in him all the sons and daughters of God.[21]

These words of Julian Hartt anticipate in theological rhetoric the argument and the proposal made by MacIntyre in philosophical terms. By the grace of God given through faithful thinking and living, we may once again recover this passion for the Gospel that is the very reason for our lives and for the church.

The Fourth Lesson

In his retrieval of the Aristotelian tradition, MacIntyre gives the church some directions for living faithfully in a fragmented world. That tradition needs considerable rethinking in the light of the Gospel. This chapter has sought to begin that process, but it can only be ultimately achieved through the lives of faithful disciples that seek the human *telos*, the living tradition, the practices and virtues of the church, and the community that lives out Hartt's call to evangelical faithfulness.

---

21. Hartt, *Toward a Theology*, 66.

SIX

The New Monasticism[1]

In the concluding paragraph of *After Virtue*, MacIntyre expresses a clear-eyed pessimism and an enigmatic hope. Warning of drawing "too precise parallels between one historical period and another," he nevertheless draws on the waning days of the Roman Empire to suggest where we may headed in Western culture. In that earlier time, he says,

> men and women of good will turned aside from the task of shoring up the Roman *imperium* and ceased to identify the continuation of civility and moral community with the maintenance of that *imperium*. What they set themselves to achieve instead— often not recognising fully what they were doing—was the construction of new forms of community within which the moral life could be sustained so that both morality and civility might survive the coming ages of barbarism and darkness. If my account of our moral condition is correct, we ought also to conclude that for some time now we too have reached that turning point. What matters at this stage is the construction of local forms of community within which civility and the intellectual and moral life can be sustained through the new dark ages which are already upon us. And if the tradition of the virtues was able to survive the horrors of the last dark ages, we are not entirely without grounds for hope. This time however the barbarians are not waiting beyond the frontiers; they have already been governing us for quite some

1. I have left the text of this chapter unchanged from the first edition in order to preserve the undeveloped thoughts that the Spirit is using to foment the rise of and connections among new monastic communities.

time. And it is our lack of consciousness of this that constitutes part of our predicament. We are waiting not for a Godot, but for another—doubtless very different—St. Benedict.[2]

I do not consider MacIntyre's pessimism to be misplaced. Indeed, the early chapters of this book are an attempt to show how the Western church is often ruled by the "new barbarians."

At the same time, I want to look with an even greater hope than MacIntyre expresses here for a "new monasticism" that will sustain, not the tradition of the virtues, but witness to the Gospel of Jesus Christ through faithful living. We can look with greater hope than MacIntyre expresses in *After Virtue*, because we look to the power of God through the Gospel to renew faithful living and witness. The new monasticism for which we look will be like the old monasticism in refusing both to shore up the *imperium* of contemporary society and to identify the future of civilization with the *imperium*. The new monasticism will be unlike the old monasticism, because the history with which we live is a different history.

Since MacIntyre concludes his book with this cryptic "prayer" for a new monasticism and leaves his prayer undeveloped, the vision that I outline for a new monasticism goes well beyond MacIntyre's book, though it draws on his argument. Moreover, since I am outlining a vision for what the church may be and not a description of what the church already is, my remarks here will be briefer than the previous chapters. What I long for is not a new St. Benedict, but Christian communities that may produce a new St. Benedict. Before I outline that vision, we must first consider MacIntyre's argument for a new monasticism.

Why a New Monasticism?

MacIntyre's call for a new monasticism, that does not seek to support or be supported by larger society, turns on his analysis of the attempts of the Jacobin clubs of the eighteenth century and Thomas Cobbett in the nineteenth century to retrieve the tradition of virtues for the whole of society. As he demonstrates, these attempts failed to achieve their goal—the Enlightenment was so entrenched in larger society that it was, and is, impossible to recover the tradition of the virtues for a whole society. Drawing on the work of Jane Austen, he shows that "both in her own

2. MacIntyre, *After Virtue*, 263.

time and afterwards, the life of the virtues is necessarily afforded a very restricted cultural and social place."[3]

What MacIntyre argues for the life of the virtues is true in a different way for the life of the church. If my critique of the life of the church in Western culture has validity, then the only way for the church to recover faithful living is for the church to disentangle its life from the culture. That is, if the church is to recover faithful living in Western culture, we must recognize the restricted cultural and social sphere within which such a recovery will take place.

However, we must be very careful in describing our reason for disentangling the life of the church from the culture. We are not to withdraw from the culture because the culture is so bad that the church cannot be a part of it. The very mission of the church calls us to be in the world as witnesses of the redemptive power of the Gospel. Nevertheless, there are times—and I have argued that this is one of them—when the life of the church has been so compromised that we no longer are capable of fulfilling faithfully our mission. At such a time, the church must withdraw into a new monasticism, not in order to avoid a bad society, but in order to recover faithful living and a renewed understanding of the church's mission.

This call to a new monasticism may sound irresponsible. Some will label such a vision "sectarian." We must recognize how much these responses depend upon the recent history of the church in Western culture. As I argued in chapter 2, the church must learn to live with its history. In Western culture, the church has long been a force in the public arena. We have been taught to think of the church as the shaper of morality, the source of values. By thinking in this way, we have allowed the life of the church to be judged by the success and progress of civilization. So any suggestion that we withdraw from a role in shaping and guiding our culture appears to be an abandonment of the mission of the church. My argument here is that however well-meant this understanding of mission is, and however successful the church has been, it is a corruption of the church's mission and life. So, given this prevalent understanding of the mission of the church and the corruption of the life of the church in Western culture, the suggestion that we need a new monasticism will indeed appear irresponsible and sectarian. However, if MacIntyre's analysis

3. MacIntyre, *After Virtue*, 243.

and my development of it in the previous chapters is correct, then for the sake of a lost and dying world we desperately need the church to recover a sense of its mission through faithful living.

The call for a new monasticism, then, is a contingent tactic, necessary in this time and place for the church to serve the world as God calls us to serve, not as the world calls us.

OUTLINE OF A NEW MONASTICISM

Therefore, we must hope, pray, and work for a new monasticism—that will, doubtless, be a very different form of life. At least four characteristics will mark this new monasticism. In some of these characteristics, the new monasticism will be continuous with the "old" monasticism; in other ways it will be discontinuous. Since we have very few examples of this new monasticism, what follows is a vision of what I think we should pray, hope, and work for, not a description of what we already have. Doubtless, if some of the people of God set to work on this vision, it will turn out very different from what anyone may imagine at this point in our history.

First, the new monasticism will be marked by *a recovery of the telos* of this world that is revealed in the Gospel of Jesus Christ. In recovering this *telos*, the new monasticism will seek to heal the fragmentation of our lives in this culture. Therefore, the new monasticism will not be marked by a division between the secular and the sacred. Rather, it will see the whole of life under the Lordship of Jesus Christ. Such an understanding will not be achieved easily or quickly, but only through great commitment and struggle. The commitment and struggle necessary for a recovery of the Gospel *telos* has little chance of occurring in the larger church. This task will be accomplished only in small, disciplined groups; in other words, in a new monastic movement.

Secondly, since this new monasticism will seek to heal the fragmentation of our culture, it will also be a monasticism *for the whole people of God*. That is, since it will not divide the world into the secular and the sacred, it will also not divide the people of God into religious and secular "vocations." Rather, it will call all of the church to live faithfully by the *telos* of the Gospel in the whole of life. Therefore, this monasticism may be lived out when a group of lawyers, teachers, business people, or others meet for lunch to consider together how their work may be ordered to the Gospel. It may be lived out as families share their lives and resources with one another. It may be lived out as church leaders consider how to expel the rule of the new barbarians—the Rich Aesthetes, Managers, and Therapists—from the life of the church.

Thirdly, since a renewed understanding of the human *telos* revealed in the Gospel is not easily or quickly achieved, the new monasticism, like the old, will be *disciplined*. However, since this discipline will be for the whole people of God, it cannot simply be a recovery of the old monastic rules. Moreover, the monastic disciplines may be easily co-opted by the mindset of the Aesthete, the Manager, and the Therapist, so that they simply become a pleasurable experience, a managerial technique, or a way to achieve peace of mind. Therefore, the church must always be careful to orient its recovery of the disciplines of the Christian life toward its *telos*. The disciplines are a means to an end: the faithful life and witness of the church.[4]

Although the new monasticism must be intended for the whole people of God, the discipline that it requires will only be achieved through small groups of disciples that are themselves committed to the vision and discipline outlined here. As I indicated above, these small groups may be oriented around particular work or life circumstances. It may also be embodied in the church by a recovery of what Dietrich Bonhoeffer calls "the arcane discipline."[5] In his cryptic remarks, Bonhoeffer seems to be calling for precisely what MacIntyre suggests: a restricted space where the church protects its life from the corruption of the world so that it can truly become, once again, the church.[6] In this arcane or "secret" discipline, the church restricts the celebration of the Eucharist to baptized believers. In this setting, the church may be more able to practice the mutual exhortation, correction, and reconciliation that marks a disciplined community.[7] Perhaps one of the reasons that the church in Western culture is not more disciplined in this sense is due to the mixed nature of the congregation that gathers for the Eucharist. In our emotivist culture, mutual exhortation and correction simply do not make sense. As a result, in most of the settings in which we celebrate the Eucharist there

---

4. Obviously, much more needs to be said here. In the present context, all that I can do is point to the work of two writers who are faithful guides to this recovery: Henri Nouwen and Eugene Peterson.

5. Bonhoeffer, *Letters and Papers*, 369–70.

6. Fowl and Jones, *Reading*, 155–57.

7. For further description of what such a community might look like, see Bonhoeffer, *Life Together*.

are powerful disincentives to the kind of discipline I am suggesting. If we are to recover faithful life and witness in the church, then in our culture we need to provide some restricted place in which the discipline of the church may be practiced. Of course, given the prevailing understanding and practice of baptism in the church, we may need to find other words to describe this restricted space.[8]

As we consider and practice this "discipline of the secret," we must also keep in mind that this separation from the world is not an abandonment of the world. Rather, it is a commitment by the church to be disciplined by the Gospel for the sake of the world, which God loves in Jesus Christ. Only in this way can the church live faithfully, witnessing to the Gospel of Jesus Christ, which is the only hope and salvation of our fragmented world.

Fourthly, the new monasticism will be undergirded by *deep theological reflection and commitment*. Only in this way can we remember the contingent, tactical purpose of the new monasticism. Here, MacIntyre's remarks may mislead us. In MacIntyre's account in *After Virtue*, the purpose of the old monasticism seems to be the provision of a place to maintain civility and the life of virtue. For the church, however, the purpose of the new monasticism is to provide the church with a means to recovering its life and witness in the world. That is, the new monasticism is not a means of protecting our children from the world, nor is it a place to learn how to be civil so that society may one day recover civility. Rather, the new monasticism provides a means by which an undisciplined and unfaithful church may recover the discipline and faithfulness necessary for its mission in the world.

Therefore, by saying that the new monasticism must be undergirded by theological commitment and reflection, I am not saying that right theology will of itself produce a faithful church. A faithful church is marked by the faithful carrying out of the mission given to the church by God in Jesus Christ, but that mission can only be identified by faithful theology. So, in the new monasticism we must strive simultaneously for a recovery of right belief and right practice.[9]

---

8. I am not thinking here of infant versus believer baptism, as much as I am thinking of the disconnection between baptism and discipleship.

9. For work that helps guide the church in this direction, in addition to the works already cited, see Saliers, *Worship*.

UNANSWERED QUESTIONS

In the preceding section, I provide only the barest sketch of a vision for a new monasticism. I am reticent to do more, because I believe a new monasticism will take shape through the gathering of committed disciples of Jesus Christ. In other words, the new monasticism that we need will not be the product of one person's vision; it will be the product of the gifts of the Holy Spirit given through many members of the body of Christ. As a result of this conviction, I have left many questions unanswered.

One unanswered question concerns the form of the new monasticism. The "old" monasticism was separated geographically, economically, and politically from the larger society. This, of course, is an overgeneralization that needs immediate qualification: the old monasticism participated in many of the pressing issues of society. Still, the question remains: How does the new monasticism separate its life from society? Should a new monastic movement establish monasteries? Should it somehow separate its economic life from that of society? I believe such questions can only be answered by particular communities as they consider their callings and their particular circumstances. I suspect that what should develop is a mixture of forms, more and less separate from society. For example, I can imagine some lawyers concluding that they can be followers of Jesus Christ only by establishing their own practices. I can imagine other lawyers concluding that they can indeed follow Jesus Christ by practicing within a larger firm. Likewise, I can imagine some establishing a new monasticism by intentionally living together and sharing a common life. I can imagine others living out a new monasticism without such arrangements.[10]

Other questions may also be left to the spiritual wisdom of particular communities and circumstances. What form should worship take? Should it be "high" church or "low" church? Should we seek to recover ancient liturgy? Should we practice the ancient monastic disciplines? What would the "simple" life look like today? These questions are vital, but I think that they are best answered in community.

As a new monastic movement considers these questions, three things must be kept in mind. First, even though they may be difficult to answer and may be divisive, such questions must be considered. Of course, we

---

10. For an insightful description of a variety of communities that provide some models and lessons for a new monasticism, see Smith, *Intimacy*.

may conclude that considerable liberty should be offered in answer to a particular question, but that liberty must be the product of spiritual struggle, not easy capitulation to our fragmented, emotivist culture. Secondly, the answers that we give must be subordinated to the larger purpose of the new monasticism—the recovery of a faithful church. Thirdly, our answers, I believe, should be placed within the context of the vision outlined above. That is, we must strive for a monasticism that does not separate the sacred and the secular, that does not distinguish among the vocations as to their ultimate *telos*, that forms disciplined communities, and that is rooted in deep theological commitment and reflection.

The Fifth Lesson

Although MacIntyre's remarks at the end of *After Virtue* are cryptic, they point the church toward the recovery of a new monasticism. This new monasticism exists today only in a few instances. In some places it is beginning to take shape. In other places it exists as a vision that has not yet been practiced.

Yet, this new monasticism is what we are called to by my use of MacIntyre to analyze the life of the church in our fragmented culture. Given the history of the church in Western culture, which I analyzed in chapter 2, we are constantly tempted to form a church that will simply undergird the civil order. A new monasticism refuses that temptation. Given our fragmented world, the church is constantly tempted to import that fragmentation into its life. A new monasticism seeks to heal that fragmentation by rediscovering the *telos* of human life revealed in the Gospel. Given the capitulation of the church to the Enlightenment project, and its consequent failure, the life of the church is constantly corrupted. A new monasticism seeks to practice a commitment and discipline that roots out that corruption and reforms the life of the church. Given the call to recovering tradition, the church needs a new form for its life that will seek and enable such a recovery. The new monasticism envisioned here is the form by which the church will recover its *telos*, the living tradition of the Gospel, the practices and virtues that sustain that faithfulness, and the community marked by faithful living in a fragmented world.

I conclude with a prayer: God grant us your Spirit, that we may have the wisdom and power to live faithfully, and so to witness to the Gospel of Jesus Christ which is the only hope of the world.

AFTERWORD[1]

In this afterword, I will offer a basic description of the new monastic movement, some reflections on the dangers that it faces, and some suggestions of the work that is yet to be done.

BASIC DESCRIPTION

It may be slightly misleading to describe what is happening as "new monasticism" or as a "new monastic movement." These descriptions may imply that there is an ideology—an "ism"—that is driving an organized movement with a clear plan for promotion and progress. But such an understanding or intention would run counter to the lessons that I have drawn from MacIntyre.

To think of new monasticism as an ideology is to misconstrue new monasticism as a phenomenon generated by this age. New monasticism is not an anti-modern ideology; nor is it a movement devised by a group of people who are anti-modern or who are seeking a way for human culture to survive the collapse of modernity and the rubble of postmodernity.

Nor is the new monastic movement the product of clever social engineering or planning. In chapters 7 and 8 of *After Virtue*, MacIntyre identifies the attractiveness that social planning holds for us in the midst of the Enlightenment project. Given the modern abandonment of *telos*, we seek control of our lives and our destinies through other means—most

1. This afterword is an opportunity for some reflection on the rise of the new monastic movement since the previous chapter was left untouched from the first edition of this book as a kind of historical artifact to represent how the vision for a new monastic movement arose from a rather undeveloped account. It should be read in conjunction with my "Introduction" to Rutba House, *School(s) for Conversion*.

commonly through social planning rooted in the social sciences. But after identifying the attractiveness of this way of life, MacIntyre shows how it cannot finally succeed.

If the rise of new monastic communities and their connections is not an ideological structure or social planning, then what is going on? Stated succinctly and in language that begs explanation and argumentation, the rise of new monastic communities is a gift of the Holy Spirit to the church and the world. This description is as much a rule for how new monastic communities are to live as it is a claim about how they have actually come to be.

As a rule for how to live, the confession that NMCs (new monastic communities) are a gift of the Holy Spirit to the church and the world means that NMCs must live their lives so as not to be captive to any ideology or to social planning. Rather, their lives and their form of life is always provisional, subject to the presence and work of the Holy Spirit. Also, their form of life is that of discernment, not planning. They are guided not by asking, "How can we accomplish our aims?" but by asking "How is God at work today and how may we participate in that work?" This latter question calls for virtues and practices that are very different from that of the former.

As a rule for how to live, this confession also teaches NMCs that they live in the church and the world for the sake of the church and the world. This conviction is rooted even more deeply in the knowledge that NMCs live in Christ, who gave himself for the life of the church and the world. NMCs live not for themselves but for Christ. And living for Christ means living for the church and world, not for oneself.

Dangers

To describe NMCs as a gift of the Holy Spirit for the church and the world may, of course, come close to and sometimes even slide into the terrible error of thinking of oneself as God's gift to the world. We may label this error *communal egotism*. Alongside this terrible error is the difficult calling to prophetic witness. Avoiding the error while fulfilling the calling is itself a constant process of failure and confession, followed by forgiveness and restoration, as well as faithfulness and thanksgiving, followed by new tasks and blessing. The way through this difficult process is located in affirming, reaffirming, and *practicing* the marks of new monasticism. These practices will keep NMCs from proclaiming themselves and focus them on proclaiming Christ. This is the prophetic way forward.

Another danger is the danger of *utopianism*. This could perhaps also be identified as idealism, but that description locates the danger too much in the cognitive rather than the practical. The two feed each other, but in the context of NMCs, utopianism is the more powerful danger and illuminating description. NMCs must not think that they are going to get it right where the "church" (really other forms of the life of the church) have gotten it wrong. Given the intentions of monastic life and the close sharing of lives in such communities, life in such communities will be more difficult in some ways than life outside such communities. Practices of confession and forgiveness, truthfulness and kindness, will be more necessary, not less. It is easy to conceal our sin individually and collectively outside intentional, close communities. If NMCs think of their way of life as easier than other ways, then they will soon fail, and in deeply hurtful ways. Forming and entering into NMCs must not be done quickly, easily, or idealistically, as if this is the solution to my pain and loneliness and lack of direction. Living in such communities may initially deepen such realities before it heals them.

Very closely related to the danger of utopianism is the danger of *romanticism*. We must not be romantics about either the old or the new monasticism. One very real danger to NMCs is the mistaken notion that the old monasticism (in whatever favorite form—Benedictine, Celtic, other) was a well-organized, clear, straightforward movement that developed in rational ways. That is simply not the case historically. Yes, we have wonderful guidance in the Rule of St. Benedict and in the monastic practices of Christian spirituality among the Celts. But those traditions developed over time and survived the test of time through the work of the Holy Spirit in the midst of a great deal of messiness and controversy and alongside many communities and practices that, in the providence of God, did not survive. NMCs must listen to critics for the guidance of the Holy Spirit, but they must not be daunted by the messiness and uncertainty of following the Spirit into a new thing. They must not romanticize the past or the present so that any failure or struggle or conflict becomes a deterrent to continuing on their calling.

Moving into a different field of dangers, we may note the temptation to *utilitarianism*. In this danger NMCs may fall into the error of thinking of their way of life as a useful way to live in a fragmented world. This danger lures us into the error of allowing our form of life to be determined by the cultural context rather than the gospel. The formation of NMCs is not a useful strategy for living well in a fragmented, emotive, cynical world. It is not a way to "make our lives better." Rather, NMCs are a way to form life faithful to the gospel. It so happens that in our contemporary "Western" setting, NMCs face the challenges and opportunities presented to faithful discipleship and witness by fragmentation, emotivism, and cynicism.

Finally we must note the danger of *Pelagianism*. This label draws on the history of theology to identify the danger of thinking that the formation and faithfulness of NMCs depends upon human ability and effort to the exclusion of God's grace. This kind of thinking is seldom explicitly adopted or endorsed, but it is regularly practiced. Its symptoms are easier to identify. They include such things as anxiety, resentment, blaming, overwork, defensiveness, Sabbath-breaking, misuse and neglect of worship, especially thanksgiving, and more.

All of these dangers, and others that I have considered elsewhere in this book—isolationism, relativism, and the Nietzschean temptation— are real dangers to NMCs. They are present among us and require us to be humble listeners to the judgment of the Holy Spirit from within our midst and outside. The practice of the "12 marks"[2] of NMCs is wonderful protection against these dangers, profound practices that expose our captivity to these dangers, and redemptive paths back to gospel faithfulness. One very helpful exercise within NMCs would be to discuss how God's grace is specifically at work in the practices of one's particular community to protect, judge, and redeem.

WORK TO DO

Part of the work to do in NMCs is simply the ongoing work of guarding against threats to faithfulness. And, in the midst of unfaithfulness, to know God's grace that judges and redeems and transforms even our unfaithfulness into a witness to Christ. Other parts of this ongoing work to do are simply the formation and maturation of NMCs.

These practices of forming and maturing are themselves susceptible to the dangers that I have identified. The formation and maturation of NMCs could be seen simply as a way of extending a movement or

2. See Rutba House, *School(s) for Conversion.*

advancing an ideology. One area of continuing discernment is to think about how publicity works to stimulate the formation of NMCs, and how it may also work against the very call of NMCs. The work and witness of NMCs is primarily local. Their life together and their witness and service depends upon geographical proximity and the visibility of their life. So at the same time that we seek to form and mature NMCs, we must do so in ways that have integrity and discern the way that the Holy Spirit is working to this end. That discernment is an ongoing practice of NMCs.

In addition to these ongoing practices, some other new or relatively new practices need attention. Among them three of the most significant tasks are the development of

- worship as central to NMCs
- a theology fitting for the life of NMCs
- a practice of Bible reading that nourishes NMCs

These are tasks to be pursued, practiced, and taught outside the limitations of this Afterword, but some direction for them may be given here.

In the context of the monastic movement throughout time, it is clear that worship has to be central to the formation and maturation of monastic communities. This practice of worship has to be shaped by the particular communities in their local settings, but it has to be central and it has to be healthy for a community to sustain life and faithfulness over time. Each of the dangers faced by NMCs is best disarmed by the practice of worship. This centrality did not play as pervasive a role in the 12 marks and their exposition as it should have. But this neglect is in the process of being corrected by the development of a prayer book for NMCs and others.[3] In addition to this prayer book, NMCs also need to discover and produce music in the context of worship and their own communal lives. They may certainly draw on music from other sources, but almost every lasting movement in the church has also generated its own music.

Another area where there is much work to be done is the discovery and exposition of a theology native to NMCs. When I read John Cassian and others in the monastic tradition, I am immediately struck by the difference in their theology as it arises from and serves the communities in which they participate. (I am also occasionally struck by how off course some monastic theology drifts.) A theology for NMCs does not mean

---

3. The title is not yet determined. The general editors are Shane Claiborne and Jonathan Wilson-Hartgrove. The publisher is Zondervan.

simply imitating or updating Cassian or another monastic theologian. Rather it means participating in NMCs with a profound fluency in the theology of the church and learning to speak and practice it in ways that are native to the life of NMCs and what God is doing in them. Such theology is not translation from one language to another but a bilingualism that enables the theologian to see God at work, hear God in a new language, and teach others to see and hear God in their own setting and language.[4]

Finally, NMCs are in the process of learning to read the Bible in new ways. They should not abandon the study and knowledge of the original languages, cultures, and histories, but those will be put in service to discerning and participating in God's work of redeeming creation. To that end, NMCs will read the Bible not primarily with historical critics or the biblical scholarship of modernity. Instead they will read the Bible primarily in a larger community that includes the excluded.[5] This community may include prisoners, the homeless, the illiterate, the poor, those who work with these, those who disobey unjust laws and protest unjust practices, as well as stockbrokers, lawyers, and everyone else. These communal readings will not be for the purpose of allowing everyone to express their feelings, their programs, their ideologies. These are not encounter groups; they are not the pooling of personal interpretations; they are not the opportunity for everyone to be heard. Rather, they are the coming together of the gifts of the Spirit so that God's work may be discerned and we may participate in it. That task is too great to be left to those with one kind of gift or training. It is a task that must be shared by the whole body of Christ in conversation with outsiders. The aim is not for everyone to be heard or for everyone to have their turn or for everyone to share their opinion. Rather, the aim is for a diversity of eyes and ears to look for and listen for God's work and voice. This aim does not eliminate or easily resolve differences and disagreements, but it does place them properly within the life of NMCs as a gift of the Holy Spirit for the church and the world.

4. For a provisional statement along these lines, see Wilson, *Why Church Matters*, chapter 5. For an example of this practice see Donovan, *Christianity Rediscovered*.

5. One of the best examples of this is Ekblad, *Reading*.

D. A. Carson on the Wilson/McLaren Post-Modern Agenda

As I noted in the Introduction, one of the oddest criticisms directed toward *Living Faithfully* is D. A. Carson's claim that "in the hands of McLaren and I . . . MacIntyre becomes a voice in defense of a post-modern agenda."[1] Carson does little to argue or explain this assertion, so I can only be tentative in responding directly to him. Moreover, Carson conflates those involved, speaking of "the MacIntyre/Wilson proposal" and "the hands of Wilson and McLaren." It should be clear from this book that I am learning from MacIntyre, but in ways that MacIntyre does not develop and of which he would not fully approve. Similarly, although I learn much from McLaren and am grateful for his vision and energy, I am not in full agreement with his work.[2] As a result of these conditions, my response here will be tentative when I directly address Carson and will become less tentative as I move to a more general and important concern that Carson's criticism rightly generates.

Carson's accusation that Wilson and McLaren use MacIntyre "in defense of a post-modern agenda" seems to be rooted in Carson's concern for truth and his perception of how we may be abandoning truth by our commitment to "Tradition." For Carson, this use of "Tradition" receives some initial approval, but then he asks, "[A]re the traditions true? Are they true

---

1. Carson, *Becoming Conversant*, 142.
2. See Wilson, *Primer*.

even for, say, educated and thoughtful Hindus who disbelieve them? Or are they our convictions just because they are our convictions?"[3]

But Carson immediately moves from these questions to "a similar debate among post-liberals." He then takes several pages to describe, interpret, and critique representatives of postliberalism such as John Franke, Hans Frei, and George Lindbeck. The connection between my supposed "post-modern agenda" (more on that below), Tradition/traditions/convictions, and postliberalism seems to be Carson's concern for "truth." Agreeing that "doctrines . . . constitute the belief mosaic of the believing community," he then asks, "[I]s what the community believes *true*?"[4] After brief further discussion, he asks, "True, the Bible conveys a 'canonical-linguistic world,' but when that canonical-linguistic world speaks of extra-canonical realities, is it speaking the truth?"[5] Carson develops his critique further, accusing postliberalism of "a merely intellectualist approach."[6] Running throughout this exposition and critique is a continuing concern for extra-textual referentiality and truth.

It might appear that Carson's concerns are extraneous to my work in *Living Faithfully*, but after these several pages he brings the argument back to my work:

> In other words, the tough questions about truth simply will not go away. Yes, we must live within the biblical narrative; yes, we fall into various Christian traditions; yes, we must learn to think holistically. But we hold that the biblical narrative is telling us the truth about what happened in history, and about God and his character and action, and about ourselves and our need, and so forth—even if it is not, and never can be, the whole truth, which is known only to the Omniscient. The Christian traditions are attempts to work out a biblical understanding, but at the end of the

3. Carson, *Becoming Conversant*, 142. My response to Carson will follow my fuller exposition of his argument, but note here that Carson has moved from "Tradition" to "traditions" to "convictions." While I would use these various terms, I would be very careful of the context and would never imagine that they are synonymous. As I will argue later, my use of "The Living Tradition" and my theological description of it are critically important to my account. Carson's critique misses that importance. As a consequence of his misreading I have tried to clarify this passage above in chapter 5, under "The Living Tradition," by adopting the language of "participating in Christ."

4. Ibid., 142–43, emphasis original.

5. Ibid., 143.

6. Ibid., 144.

day they must be revisable in the light of Scripture, which is what
God himself has given. On none of these matters is the emerging church movement very clear. So loathe are some members
to talk at length about truth (even though Scripture as we shall
see, shares none of these inhibitions) that appeals like Wilson's to
live out a tradition keep ducking the tough question: *Why* should
we live out this tradition? Because we were born into it? Because
we find it more coherent than others? Because the notion of self-
sacrifice is attractive? Or will we allow space for the apostolic in-
sistence on truth?[7]

Although Carson seems to be addressing a number of different issues, it
does seem that the underlying concern in this section is my use of "tradition." But there are other issues woven into his exposition and argument that also have to be untangled and addressed. At one level, Carson's
exposition is so tangled that direct engagement is perhaps unnecessary.
But the issues he weaves together are also important to me and can be
misconstrued so that I could fail in my aim to help the church live faithfully in a fragmented world.

In my response, I will focus carefully on what I have tried to teach
and argue. I will set aside Carson's conflation of my views with McLaren
and MacIntyre, though I may occasionally refer to their work. I will not
try to answer for them, nor will I be drawn into defending McLaren simply because he uses some of my work in his own. I will address three
issues: my supposed "post-modern agenda"; the relation of truth and
tradition; the character of postliberal theology.

Recall that Carson suggests that I turn MacIntyre into "a voice in
defense of a post-modern agenda." Carson does not explain this further,
though it may have something to do with his subsequent questions about
truth. Lacking any clear and direct explanation of the accusation from
Carson, let me simply state where I stand on the question of a "post-
modern agenda." Most of what I am going to say here has already been

---

7. Ibid., 145–46. I have quoted Carson at length in order to set before the reader
his full exposition and argument before analyzing and critiquing it. That my work is in
Carson's view throughout this section is further indicated by the fact that Carson ends
with a footnote that begins, "There are several other problems with Wilson's 'take' on
MacIntyre that would lead us outside the purpose of this book. I briefly mention one
of them." He goes on to identify my call to "a new monasticism" as a call to a "separatist
community, a sort of updated Anabaptist community." Ibid., 146 n. 41. I address this
criticism in my Introduction above.

clearly and more fully developed in the running critique of postmodernity throughout my book *Gospel Virtues*.

To the extent that I have any "post-modern agenda," it is a missionary agenda. I want to understand the particular culture in which we are called to bear witness to the gospel, so that we may do so with the greatest faithfulness possible under the guidance of the Holy Spirit. To that end, I am convinced that "postmodern" is an instructive description of the changing culture in which we find ourselves. I also find many insights in postmodern theorists, whom I regard as a class of anthropologists studying a particular culture. I have absolutely no interest in advancing or celebrating the culture of postmodernity. I am deeply committed to understanding it, so that I know how it offers both threats to and opportunities for faithfully living out and witnessing to the gospel. That is the only "post-modern agenda" that I am consciously committed to; I am sure that given my own history I am unaware of ways in which postmodernity shapes me and distorts my faithfulness to the gospel. That is why I need new monastic communities to help me.

It may be that Carson's concern for my "post-modern agenda" is tied to his description of my affirmation of "Tradition." Recall here that Carson glides from "Tradition" to "traditions" to "convictions." These connections are not entirely unfair, but they do miss the substance of my account and lead to criticisms that miss the mark. In my account (above, chapter 5) I write about "The Living Tradition." This is a reality different from the tradition versus Scripture controversy that has marked much of Christian history. I nowhere in my exposition use the language of traditions. As was my way of working with these concepts from MacIntyre, I begin with his exposition, remembering that in *After Virtue* his constructive account is Aristotelian not Christian. After a brief exposition of his work and an acknowledgement that his account requires further development, I then give a Christian alternative. Here is how I describe that alternative:

> [I]n the Gospel the church not only encounters a living tradition but an ever-present reality. That is, the Gospel is not merely something from the past that continues to live on in the memory of the church; it is also, and more significantly, the redeeming work of God in Jesus Christ present in the past and present today. The church's calling is to discern that present reality and live faithfully

in it. Thus, the life of the church embodies the rationality of the Gospel.

In a church marked by the moral fragmentation of the Enlightenment project, such an outcome cannot occur. But in a church that is seeking to be faithful to a living tradition under the guidance of the Holy Spirit, such an outcome is promised.

To take MacIntyre's words captive for the gospel, we may say that the church is "an historically-extended, socially embodied argument" for the truth of the gospel.

But truth is precisely what Carson is so concerned about. Here in Carson's account I think that we have yet another example of the struggle for us to understand one another across cultural divides. For Carson, it seems (I state tentatively) that the truth of the gospel must correspond to something external to the gospel. I am not sure that is the case and I have not found another place where Carson makes this clear.

So rather than critique or continue to suppose what Carson means by truth, I will make two observations preliminary to my brief account of truth. (I recognize the potential folly of giving a "brief account of truth"!) First, we all need to recognize that "truth" is an equivocal term whose meaning is profoundly shaped by our history and culture. So just because someone does not give an account of truth that looks and sounds like mine, does not mean that they have no concern for, or account of, truth. Secondly, my teacher Julian Hartt, in one of his later unpublished pieces, issues a call for theologians and others to pursue the intellectual discipline of alethiology, the study of truth. This pursuit would be so much more fitting and delightful than epistemology or ontology, though I am sure it would not take too long for us to professionalize it and drain it of life.

With those acknowledgements, I can now turn to the question of truth. Carson is right in his understanding of my argument if he thinks that I am giving an account of truth that differs from "the standard account." But if he thinks that I have no concern for the truth of the gospel, then he is wrong. I am almost certain that we disagree on the best way to give an account of the truth of the gospel. And I may be wrong in my account, but to say that I have no interest in the truth of the gospel or no account of the truth is a misreading of my work. In my account of the failure of the Enlightenment project I write:

Before we move on to consider the consequences of this failure, we should consider an objection, often directed toward MacIntyre, that may be brought against my account. To some, MacIntyre's account, and by extension my account, may appear to give no means for judging among competing convictions and traditions. In other words, our accounts appear fideistic or relativistic. However, as MacIntyre shows in a later work (MacIntyre 1989), his position does allow for rational comparison. Moreover, James Wm. McClendon Jr. and James M. Smith have given an extensive account of evaluating and justifying religious convictions that is compatible with the position I am advocating (McClendon and Smith, *Convictions*). What our accounts preclude is the notion that there are grounds for justifying the Gospel apart from the Gospel itself.

To go beyond MacIntyre's account, the way for the church to justify the claims of the Gospel is by living the way of life to which the Gospel calls us. This way of life, as it displays the full claims of the Gospel, may then be compared to other ways of life. This comparison occurs, not from some Archimedean point outside every tradition, but from within one's present tradition as one considers the competing claims. In this understanding, the church commends the Gospel by living according to the Gospel, not by appealing to some ground outside the Gospel. For this very reason then, this work is about *living faithfully* in a fragmented world: living faithfully simply *is* the Christian mission in the modern world.[8]

And in the context of my exposition of "The Living Tradition," the very passage that concerns Carson, I write that one "lesson we must learn from MacIntyre's account of a living tradition is the rationality of tradition over against other forms of rationality."[9] MacIntyre develops his insights in *Whose Justice? Which Rationality?*; *Three Rival Versions of Moral Enquiry*; and *Dependent Rational Animals*. The second may be particularly helpful. Although MacIntyre is focused on moral enquiry, he really identifies three forms of rationality: encyclopedia, genealogy, and tradition. The encyclopedia represents modernity, genealogy represents postmodernity, and tradition represents, well, another form.

Each of these also represents an understanding of truth. They have competing understandings, but each has one that is pursued with rigor.

8. Wilson, *Living Faithfully* (1997), 45.
9. Ibid., 60.

It seems to me from Carson's text that he works with an encyclopedist's understanding of truth. I say this because of his concern for "external reference" in regard to the truth of the teaching of Scripture. But he may be closer to "tradition" than he recognizes. It really turns on what he means when he asks for "extra-textual referentiality."[10]

Carson's call for extra-textual referentiality may mean that the teaching of Scripture may only be proven true by evidence gathered by means apart from that to which the Scripture bears witness—by, say, archaeological digs, historical investigations, scientific experiments, philosophical reflection. If this is what he means, then he has adopted "the standard account of truth" that, ironically, regards archaeology, history, science, and philosophy as more authoritative than the gospel because the gospel may be shown as true only by appeal to one of these extra-textual references.

However, Carson's call for extra-textual referentiality may mean that we must see that the claims of Scripture about God's work of redemption in Christ are real. That is, it is not enough to say that the Bible declares it; we must also see the actuality of God's redemption. If this is what he means, then he is really articulating the "rationality" and the "truth" of the living tradition which is the reality of God's work of redemption in Christ. To appeal to something outside the reality of God's work in order to prove the truth of that work is to grant greater authority to that "outside" than to the gospel. Again, this is not fideism or relativism; this is gospel reality, gospel knowing, gospel arguing, gospel witnessing, gospel truth.[11]

Finally, we consider postliberal theology. First, I must warn that postliberal theology has no investment in postmodernity or a postmodern agenda. Its history is almost entirely tied to modernity. At the 1995 Wheaton Theology Conference, George Lindbeck described postliberal theology as a research project intended to recover a pre-modern way of reading the Bible. Another way to describe the postliberal project is to say that it is an attempt to commend the truth of the gospel, not by practices extrinsic to the gospel, such as scientific history, historical-critical interpretation, or philosophical reason, but by practices intrinsic to the gospel, such as the witness of the church, lives of discipleship, and interpreting the world according to Scripture. This is the commitment of postliberal theology precisely because it recognizes, with Carson, that the gospel is

10. Carson, *Becoming Conversant*, 145.

11. Much more could be said here. I hope to address this issue at greater length in a book tentatively titled *Gospel and Theology*.

not an idea or set of ideas but the reality of God's work of redeeming creation through Jesus Christ.

It is the case that Lindbeck and others have made confusing and misleading statements. Most of these—and especially the ones that Carson picks on—have been acknowledged and clarified in subsequent debate.[12] Moreover, Carson, after listing a number of concerns about the truth of the biblical narrative, is right in claiming that "on none of these matters is the emerging church movement very clear." He also is right to claim that members of the emerging church movement are loathe "to talk at length about truth."[13] I have aimed here to bring some clarity to these topics. I have identified some better ways of understanding and thinking about the matters that so concern Carson because they also concern me. It is important that we are guided by the living tradition—the reality of the gospel in which we participate by the Holy Spirit—as we follow a process of communal discernment in order to live faithfully in a fragmented world.[14]

12. Marshall, *Theology* and *Trinity*.

13. Carson, *Becoming Conversant*, 145.

14. See my further writings on the topics covered in this Appendix in Wilson *Theology; God So Loved; Old Testament.*

Bonhoeffer, Dietrich. *Letters and Papers from Prison.* Translated by Reginald Fuller et al. Edited by Eberhard Bethge. New York: Macmillan, 1972.

———. *Life Together.* Translated by John W. Doberstein. New York: Harper & Row, 1954.

Braght, Thielman J. van. *The Bloody Theatre, or Martyrs Mirror of the Defenseless Christians.* Scottdale, PA: Herald, 1998 [1660].

Carson, D. A. *Becoming Conversant with the Emerging Church: Understanding a Movement and Its Implications.* Grand Rapids: Zondervan, 2005.

Carter, Craig A. *Rethinking Christ and Culture: A Post-Christendom Perspective.* Grand Rapids: Brazos, 2006.

Donvan, Vincent J. *Christianity Rediscovered.* 25th anniv. ed. Maryknoll, NY: Orbis, 2003.

Dyrness, William A. *How Does America Hear the Gospel?* Grand Rapids: Eerdmans, 1989.

Ekblad, Bob. *Reading the Bible with the Damned.* Louisville: Westminster John Knox, 2005.

Fowl, Stephen E., and L. Gregory Jones. *Reading in Communion: Scripture and Ethics in Christian Life.* Grand Rapids: Eerdmans, 1991.

Frei, Hans W. *The Eclipse of Biblical Narrative: A Study in Eighteenth and Nineteenth Century Hermeneutics.* New Haven: Yale University Press, 1980.

———. *Theology and Narrative: Selected Essays.* Edited by George Hunsinger. New York: Oxford University Press, 1993.

———. *Types of Christian Theology.* New Haven: Yale University Press, 1992.

Gustafson, James M. "Preface: An Appreciative Interpretation." In *Christ and Culture,* by H. Richard Niebuhr, xxi–xxxv. 50th anniv. ed. San Francisco: HarperSanFrancisco, 2001.

Hartt, Julian N. *A Christian Critique of American Culture: An Essay in Practical Theology.* New York: Harper & Row, 1967.

———. *Toward a Theology of Evangelism.* New York: Abingdon, 1955.

Hauerwas, Stanley. *After Christendom? How the Church Is to Behave If Freedom, Justice, and a Christian Nation Are Bad Ideas.* Nashville: Abingdon, 1991.

———. *Character and the Christian Life: A Study in Theological Ethics.* San Antonio: Trinity University Press, 1975.

Hauerwas, Stanley, and Charles Robert Pinches. *Christians among the Virtues: Theological Conversations with Ancient and Modern Ethics.* Notre Dame: University of Notre Dame Press, 1997.

Hauerwas, Stanley, and William H. Willimon. *Resident Aliens: Life in the Christian Colony.* Nashville: Abingdon, 1989.

Horton, John, and Susan Mendus. *After MacIntyre: Critical Perspectives on the Work of Alasdair MacIntyre.* Notre Dame: University of Notre Dame Press, 1994.

Jones, L. Gregory. *Embodying Forgiveness: A Theological Analysis.* Grand Rapids: Eerdmans, 1995.

————. *Transformed Judgment: Toward a Trinitarian Account of the Moral Life.* Notre Dame: University of Notre Dame Press, 1990.

Kallenberg, Brad J. *Live to Tell: Evangelism in a Postmodern World.* Grand Rapids: Brazos, 2002.

Kallenberg, Brad J., et al. *Virtues & Practices in the Christian Tradition: Christian Ethics after Macintyre.* Notre Dame: University of Notre Dame Press, 2003.

Kimball, Dan. *They Like Jesus but Not the Church: Insights from Emerging Generations.* Grand Rapids: Zondervan, 2007.

MacIntyre, Alasdair C. *After Virtue: A Study in Moral Theory.* 1st ed. London: Duckworth, 1981.

————. *After Virtue: A Study in Moral Theory.* 2nd ed. Notre Dame: University of Notre Dame Press, 1984.

————. *After Virtue: A Study in Moral Theory.* 3rd ed. Notre Dame: University of Notre Dame Press, 2007.

————. *Dependent Rational Animals: Why Human Beings Need the Virtues.* Chicago: Open Court, 1999.

————. *Three Rival Versions of Moral Enquiry: Encyclopedia, Genealogy, and Tradition: Being Gifford Lectures Delivered in the University of Edinburgh in 1988.* University of Notre Dame Press, 1990.

————. *Whose Justice? Which Rationality?* Notre Dame: University of Notre Dame Press, 1988.

Marsden, George. *The Soul of the American University: From Protestant Establishment to Established Unbelief.* New York: Oxford University Press, 1994.

Marshall, Bruce. *Theology and Dialogue: Essays in Conversation with George Lindbeck.* Notre Dame: University of Notre Dame Press, 1990.

————. *Trinity and Truth.* New York: Cambridge University Press, 2000.

McClendon, James Wm. Jr. *Ethics: Systematic Theology.* Nashville: Abingdon, 1986.

McClendon, James Wm. Jr., and James M. Smith. *Convictions: Defusing Religious Relativism.* Valley Forge, PA: Trinity, 1994.

Milbank, John. *Theology and Social Theory.* Oxford: Blackwell, 1990.

Newbigin, Lesslie. *Foolishness to the Greeks: The Gospel and Western Culture.* Grand Rapids: Eerdmans, 1986.

————. *The Gospel in a Pluralist Society.* Grand Rapids: Eerdmans, 1989.

————. *Truth to Tell: The Gospel as Public Truth.* Grand Rapids: Eerdmans, 1991.

Plantinga, Cornelius Jr. *Not the Way It's Supposed to Be.* Grand Rapids: Eerdmans, 1995.

Rawls, John. *Political Liberalism.* New York: Columbia University Press, 1993.

Rutba House. *School(s) for Conversion: 12 Marks for a New Monasticism.* Eugene, OR: Cascade, 2005.

Saliers, Don E. *Worship as Theology: Foretaste of Glory Divine.* Nashville: Abingdon, 1994.

Schuller, Robert. *Self-Esteem: The New Reformation.* Dallas: Word, 1985.

Smith, Luther E. *Intimacy and Mission: Intentional Community as Crucible for Radical Discipleship.* Scottdale, PA: Herald, 1994.

Stackhouse, John G. *Making the Best of It: Following Christ in the Real World*. New York: Oxford University Press, 2008.

Stassen, Glen Harold, et al. *Authentic Transformation: A New Vision of Christ and Culture*. Nashville: Abingdon, 1996.

Stone, Bryan P. *Evangelism after Christendom: The Theology and Practice of Christian Witness*. Grand Rapids: Brazos, 2007.

Tilley, Terrence W. "In Favor of a 'Practical Theory of Religion.'" In *Theology without Foundations: Religious Practice and the Future of Theological Truth*, edited by Stanley Hauerwas et al., 49–74. Nashville: Abingdon, 1994.

Wilson, Jonathan R. *Living Faithfully in a Fragmented World: Lessons for the Church from Macintyre's After Virtue*. Harrisburg, PA: Trinity, 1997.

———. "Living Faithfully in a Fragmented World: Four Lessons for the Church from MacIntyre's *After Virtue*." *CRUX* 4 (1990) 38–42.

———. *God So Loved the World: A Christology for Disciples*. Grand Rapids: Baker, 2001.

———. *Gospel Virtues: Practicing Faith, Hope, and Love in Uncertain Times*. Eugene, OR: Wipf & Stock, 2006.

———. "Old Testament Narrative and Christian Ethics." In *The Bible in World Christian Perspective: Studies in Honor of Carl Edwin Armerding*, edited by David Baker and Ward Gasque, 165–74. Regent College Publishing, 2009.

———. *A Primer for Christian Doctrine*. Grand Rapids: Eerdmans, 2005.

———. *Theology as Cultural Critique: The Achievement of Julian Hartt*. Macon, GA: Mercer University Press, 1996.

———. *Why Church Matters: Worship, Ministry, and Mission in Practice*. Grand Rapids: Brazos, 2006.

Yoder, John Howard. *The Priestly Kingdom: Social Ethics as Gospel*. Notre Dame: University of Notre Dame Press, 1984.